CAMBRIDGE LIBRA

Books of enduring ;

Women's Writing

The later twentieth century saw a huge wave of academic interest in women's writing, which led to the rediscovery of neglected works from a wide range of genres, periods and languages. Many books that were immensely popular and influential in their own day are now studied again, both for their own sake and for what they reveal about the social, political and cultural conditions of their time. A pioneering resource in this area is Orlando: Women's Writing in the British Isles from the Beginnings to the Present (http://orlando.cambridge.org), which provides entries on authors' lives and writing careers, contextual material, timelines, sets of internal links, and bibliographies. Its editors have made a major contribution to the selection of the works reissued in this series within the Cambridge Library Collection, which focuses on non-fiction publications by women on a wide range of subjects from astronomy to biography, music to political economy, and education to prison reform.

The Land Beyond the Forest

Novelist Emily Gerard (1849–1905) went with her husband, an officer in the Austrian army, to Transylvania for two years in 1883. Then part of the Austro-Hungarian Empire, today a region of western Romania, Transylvania was little known to readers back in England. In the years following, she wrote this full-length account (published in 1888) as well as several articles on the region, which Bram Stoker used when researching the setting for *Dracula*. She describes her encounters with the different nationalities that made up the Transylvanian people: Romanians, Saxons and gypsies. Full of startling anecdotes and written in a novelistic style, her work combines her personal recollections with a detailed account of the landscape and people. The first volume recounts her first impressions and the superstitions and customs of the Romanian and Saxon populations.For more information on this author, see http://orlando.cambridge.org/public/svPeople?person_id=geraem

Cambridge University Press has long been a pioneer in the reissuing of out-of-print titles from its own backlist, producing digital reprints of books that are still sought after by scholars and students but could not be reprinted economically using traditional technology. The Cambridge Library Collection extends this activity to a wider range of books which are still of importance to researchers and professionals, either for the source material they contain, or as landmarks in the history of their academic discipline.

Drawing from the world-renowned collections in the Cambridge University Library, and guided by the advice of experts in each subject area, Cambridge University Press is using state-of-the-art scanning machines in its own Printing House to capture the content of each book selected for inclusion. The files are processed to give a consistently clear, crisp image, and the books finished to the high quality standard for which the Press is recognised around the world. The latest print-on-demand technology ensures that the books will remain available indefinitely, and that orders for single or multiple copies can quickly be supplied.

The Cambridge Library Collection will bring back to life books of enduring scholarly value (including out-of-copyright works originally issued by other publishers) across a wide range of disciplines in the humanities and social sciences and in science and technology.

The Land
Beyond the Forest

Facts, Figures, and Fancies from Transylvania

VOLUME 1

EMILY GERARD

CAMBRIDGE
UNIVERSITY PRESS

CAMBRIDGE UNIVERSITY PRESS

Cambridge, New York, Melbourne, Madrid, Cape Town, Singapore,
São Paolo, Delhi, Dubai, Tokyo, Mexico City

Published in the United States of America by Cambridge University Press, New York

www.cambridge.org
Information on this title: www.cambridge.org/9781108021609

© in this compilation Cambridge University Press 2010

This edition first published 1888
This digitally printed version 2010

ISBN 978-1-108-02160-9 Paperback

OLD TOWN GATE AT HERMANSTADT.

ELISABETH THOR.

PHOTOGRAPHED BY MADAME KAMILLA ASBOTH, HERMANSTADT.

THE

LAND BEYOND THE FOREST

FACTS, FIGURES, AND FANCIES

FROM TRANSYLVANIA

BY

E. GERARD

AUTHOR OF ' REATA,' ' THE WATERS OF HERCULES,' ETC.

With Map and Illustrations

IN TWO VOLUMES—VOL. I.

WILLIAM BLACKWOOD AND SONS
EDINBURGH AND LONDON
MDCCCLXXXVIII

PREFACE.

In the spring of 1883 my husband was appointed to the command of the cavalry brigade in Transylvania, composed of two hussar regiments, stationed respectively at Hermanstadt and Kronstadt,—a very welcome nomination, as gratifying a long-cherished wish of mine to visit that part of the Austrian empire known as the Land beyond the Forest.

The two years spent in Transylvania were among the most agreeable of sixteen years' acquaintance with Austrian military life ; and I shall always look back to this time as to something quaint and exceptional, totally different from all previous and subsequent experiences.

Much interested in the wild beauty of the country, the strange admixture of races by which it is peopled, and their curious and varied folk-lore, I recorded some of my impressions in short inde-

pendent papers, of which three appeared in 'Blackwood's Magazine,' one in the 'Nineteenth Century,' and one in the 'Contemporary Review.' It
was only after I had left the country, that, being
desirous of preserving these sketches in more convenient form, I began rearranging the matter for
publication. But the task of retracing my Transylvanian experiences was so pleasant that it led
me on far beyond my original intention; one
reminiscence awoke another, one chapter gave rise
to a second; and so, instead of one small volume, as
had been at first contemplated, my manuscript
almost unconsciously developed to its present
dimensions.

When the work was completed, the idea of illus-
trating it occurred to me : but this was a far more
difficult matter ; for, though offering a perfect treas-
ure-mine to artists, Transylvania has not as yet
received from them the attention it deserves; and
had it not been for obliging assistance from several
quarters, I should have been debarred the satisfaction of elucidating some of my descriptions by
appropriate sketches.

In this matter my thanks are greatly due to
Herr Emil Sigerus, who was good enough to place
at my disposal the blocks of engravings designed
by himself, and belonging to the Transylvanian

Carpathian Society, of which he is the secretary. Likewise to Madame Kamilla Asboth, for permission to copy her lifelike and characteristic photographs of Saxons, Roumanians, and gipsies.

I would also at this place acknowledge the extreme courtesy with which every question of mine regarding Transylvanian people and customs has been responded to by various kind acquaintances, and if some parts of my work do not meet with their entire approval, let them here take the assurance that my remarks were prompted by no unfriendly spirit, and that in each and every case I have endeavoured to judge impartially according to my lights.

E. DE L. G.

VIENNA, *February* 1888.

CONTENTS OF THE FIRST VOLUME.

ILLUSTRATIONS OF THE FIRST VOLUME.

THE LAND BEYOND THE FOREST.

CHAPTER I.

INTRODUCTORY.

LEAVING Transylvania after a two years' residence, I felt somewhat like Robinson Crusoe unexpectedly restored to the world from his desert island. Despite the evidence of my own senses, and in flat contradiction to the atlas, I cannot wholly divest myself of the idea that it is in truth an island I have left behind me—an island peopled with strange and incongruous companions, from whom I part with a mixture of regret and relief, difficult to explain even to myself.

Just as Robinson Crusoe, getting attached to his parrots and his palm-trees, his gourds and his goats, continued to yearn for them after his return to Europe, so I found myself gradually succumbing to the indolent charm and the drowsy poetry of this secluded land. A very few years more of unbroken residence here, would no doubt suffice to efface all memory of the world we had left behind, and the century in which we live.

I remember reading in some fairy tale long ago, of a youthful princess who, stolen by the gnomes and carried off into gnomeland, was restored to her parents after a lapse of years. Their joy was great at recovering their child, but it turned to grief when they discovered that she had grown estranged from them, and had lost all interest in the actual world. The sun was too bright, she said, it hurt her eyes, and the voices of men were too loud, they scorched her ears; and she could never feel at home again amid the restless glitter of her surroundings.

I do not recollect how the story concludes,—whether the young lady became in time reconciled to her father's brilliant court, or whether she ran away and married a gnome; but this tale somehow reminded me of my own experiences, and I caught myself wondering whether a few years hence, perhaps, the summons to return to the world might not have come too late.

Parrots and palm-trees are all very well, no doubt, to fill up the life of a stranded mariner, but it is questionable whether it be wise to let such things absorb the mind to the extent of destroying all taste for wider interests. Life in an island is apt to consist too entirely of foreground—the breadth of a panorama and the comprehensiveness of a bird's-eye view, only gained by constant friction with the bustling, pushing outer world, being mostly here wanting.

Luckily, or unluckily, as one may choose to view it, the spirit of the nineteenth century is a ghost very difficult to be laid. A steady course of narcotics may lull it to rest for a time; but the spirit is but stupefied, not dead: its vitality is great, and it will start up again to life at the first trumpet-blast which reaches from without, eager to exchange a peaceful dream for the movement of the arena and the renewed clank of arms.

Some such feelings were mine as I beheld the signal waving from the ship which was to carry me back to a world I had almost forgotten; and though I heaved a sigh of regret, and possibly may have dropped a tear or two in secret for the peaceful and familiar scenes I was leaving, yet I would not have steered round the vessel to return to my island.

Not the mere distance which separates Transylvania from Western Europe gives to it this feeling

of strange isolation.   Other countries as far or
farther off are infinitely more familiar even to
those who have never visited them.   We know
all about Turkey, and Greece is no more strange
to us than Italy or Switzerland.   But no one ever
comes to Transylvania in cold blood, unless it be
some very rabid sportsman eager for the embrace
of a shaggy bear ; and as for those rushing travel-
lers, bound for the Black Sea, who sometimes
traverse the country in hot-headed haste, they
mostly resemble the superficial swallow which
skims the surface of a placid lake, without guessing the secrets of the blue depths below.

Situated by nature within a formidable rampart
of snow-tipped mountains, and shielded by heavy
curtains of shrouding forests against the noise and
turmoil of the outer world, the very name of
Transylvania tells us that it was formerly regarded
as something apart, something out of reach, whose
existence even for a time was enveloped in mys-
tery.   In olden times these gloomy forest-gorges
were tenanted only by the solitary bear or packs
of famished wolves, while the mistrustful lynx
looked down from the giddy heights, and the
chamois leaped unchecked from rock to rock.   The
people who lived westward of this mountain rampart, knowing but little or nothing of the country
on the other side, designated it as Transylvania or

the land beyond the forest, just as we sometimes talk of the "land beyond the clouds."

Nothing, however, can remain undiscovered on the face of our globe. That enterprising creature man, who is even now attempting, with some show of success, to probe the country beyond the clouds, has likewise discovered the way to this secluded nook. The dense forests, once forming such impenetrable barrier against the outer world, have in great part disappeared; another voice is heard beside that of the wild beasts of the wood; another breath comes mingled along with the mountain vapours—it is the breath of that nineteenth-century monster, the steam-engine.

This benefactor of the age, this harbinger of civilisation, which is as truly the destroyer of romance, and poetry's deadly foe, will undoubtedly succeed in robbing this country of the old-world charm which yet lingers about it. Transylvania will in time become as civilised and cultivated, and likewise as stereotyped and conventional, as the best-known parts of our first European states,—it will even one day cease to be an island; but as yet the advent of the nineteenth-century monster is of too recent a date to have tainted the atmosphere by its breath, and the old-world charm still lingers around and about many things. It is floating everywhere and anywhere—in the forests and on the mountains, in medieval churches and ruined watch-towers, in mysterious caverns and in ancient gold-mines, in the songs of the people and the legends they tell. Like a subtle perfume evaporating under the rays of a burning sun, it is growing daily fainter and fainter, and all lovers of the past should hasten to collect this fleeting fragrance ere it be gone for ever. This is what I have endeavoured to do, to some small extent, since fate for a time cast my lines in those parts.

And first and foremost let me here explain that my intentions in compiling these volumes are no-wise of an ambitious or lofty nature. I desire to instruct no one, to influence no one, to enlist no one's sympathies in favour of any particular social question or political doctrine. Even had such been my intention, I have been therein amply forestalled by others; nor do I delude myself into the belief that it is my proud vocation to correct the errors of all former writers by giving to the world the only correct and trustworthy description of Transylvania which has yet appeared. I have not lived long enough in the country to feel my-self justified in taking up the gauntlet against the assertions of older inhabitants of the soil, but have lived there too long to rival that admirable self-possession which induces the average tourist to classify, condemn, ticket and tie up, every fact which comes within his notice, never demeaning himself to grovel or analyse, nor being disturbed by any doubts of the reliability of his own unerring judgment.

Whoever wishes to study the history of Transylvania in its past, present, and future aspects, who wants to understand its geological formation or system of agriculture, who would thoroughly penetrate into the inextricable network of conflicting political interests which divide its interior, must seek his information elsewhere.

Do you wish, for instance, to see Transylvania as it was some forty years ago? If so, I can confidently advise you to read the valuable work of Mr Paget and the spirited descriptions of Monsieur de Gérando.

Do you want to gain insight into the geological resources of the country, or the farming system of the Saxon peasant? then take up Charles Boner's comprehensive work on Transylvania; and would you see these Saxons as they love to behold themselves, then turn to Dr Teutsch's learned work on 'Die Siebenbürger Sachsen'; while if politics be your special hobby, you cannot better indulge it than by selecting Mr Patterson's most interesting work on Hungary and Transylvania.

If, moreover, you care to study the country "contrariwise," and would know what the Rou-

manians are utterly unlike, read the description of
them in the aforementioned book of Mr Boner;
while for generally incorrect information on almost
every available subject connected with the country,
I am told that the German work of Rudolf Bergner
cannot be too highly recommended.

Recognising, therefore, the superiority of the
many learned predecessors who each in their respective lives have so thoroughly worked out the
subject in hand, I would merely forewarn the
reader that no such completeness of outline can
be looked for here. Neither is my book intended
to be of the guide-book species—no sort of orna-
mental Bradshaw or idealised Murray. I fail to
see the use of minutely describing several score of
towns and villages which the English reader is
never likely to set eyes upon. If you think of
travelling this way, good and well, then buy the
genuine article for yourself—Murray or Bradshaw
—unadulterated by me; or better still, the excellent German handbook of Professor Bielz: while
if you stay at home, can you really care to
know if such and such a town have five churches
or fifty? or whether the proportion of carbonate
of magnesia exceed that of chloride of potassium
in some particular spring of whose waters you will
never taste?

All that I have attempted here to do is to seize

the general colour and atmosphere of the land, and to fix—as much for my own private satisfaction as for any other reason—certain impressions of people and places I should be loath to forget. I have only written of those things which happened to excite my interest, and have described figures and scenery such as they appeared to me. For some of the details contained in these pages I am indebted to the following writers: Liszt, Slavici, Fronius, Müller, and Schwicker — all competent authorities well acquainted with their subject. Some things have found no place here, because I did not consider myself competent to speak of them, others because they did not chance to be congenial; and although not absolutely scorning serious information whenever it has come in my way, I have taken more pleasure in chronicling fancies than facts, and superstitions rather than statistics.

More than one error has doubtless crept unawares into this work; so in order to place myself quite on the safe side with regard to stern critics, I had better hasten to say that I decline to pledge my word for the veracity of anything contained in these pages. I only lay claim to having used my eyes and ears to the best of my ability; and where I have failed to see or hear aright, the fault must be set down to some inherent colour-blindness, or radical defect in my tympanum. Nor do I pretend to have seen everything, even in a small country like Transylvania; and every spot I have failed to visit, from lack of time or opportunity, is not only to me a source of poignant regret, but likewise a chapter missing from this book.

CHAPTER II.

TRANSYLVANIA is interesting not only on account
of its geographical position, but likewise with regard to the several races which inhabit it, and the
peculiar conditions under which part of these have
obtained possession of the soil.

Situated between 45° 16′ and 48° 42′ latitude,
and 40° to 44° of longitude (Ferro), the land covers
a space of 54,000 square kilometres, which are
inhabited by a population of some 2,170,000
heads.

Of these, the proportion of different races may
be assumed to be pretty nearly as follows :—

Roumanians, ...	1,200,400
Hungarians, ...	652,221
Saxons, ...	211,490
Gipsies, ...	79,000
Jews, ...	24,848
Armenians, ...	8,430

Some one has rather aptly defined Transylvania

as a vast storehouse of different nationalities; and in order to account for the *raison d'être* of so many different races living side by side in one small country, a few words of explanation are absolutely necessary to render intelligible the circumstances of daily life in Transylvania, since it is to be presumed that to many English readers the country is still virtually a "land beyond the forest."

Not being, however, of that ferocious disposition which loves to inflict needless information upon an unoffending public, I pass over in considerate silence such very superfluous races as the Agathyrsi, the Gepidæ, the Getæ, and yet others who successively inhabited these regions. Let it suffice to say, that in the centuries immediately preceding the Christian era the land belonged to the Dacians, who were in course of time subjugated by Trajan, — Transylvania becoming a Roman province in the year 105 A.D. It remained under the Roman eagle for something over a century and a half; but about the year 274, the Emperor Aurelian was compelled to remove his legions from the countries over the Danube, and abandon the land to the all-ravaging Goths.

I have only here insisted on the Dacian and Roman occupation of Transylvania, because one or other or both of these people are supposed to be the ancestors of the present Roumanian race. The Roumanians themselves like to think they are descended directly from the Romans; while Germans are fond of denying this origin, and maintain this people to have appeared in these regions at a much later period. According to the most reliable authorities, however, the truth would seem to lie between these two opposite statements, and the Roumanians to be the offspring of a cross-breed between the conqueror and the conquered—between Romans and Dacians.

After the Roman evacuation the country changed hands oftener than can be recorded, and the rolling waves of the *Völkerwanderung* passed over the land, each nation leaving its impress more or less upon the surface, till finally the Magyars began to gain something of a permanent hold towards the eleventh century. This hold, however, was anything but a firm one, for the Hungarian king had alike outward enemies and inward traitors to guard against, and was in continual fear lest some affectionate relation should rob him of one of his crown jewels.

To add to this, the province of Transylvania was but thinly peopled, and ill qualified to resist attacks from without. In view, therefore, of all these circumstances, King Geisa II. bethought himself of inviting Germans to come and establish colonies in

this scantily-peopled land, promising them certain
privileges in return for the services he expected.

Hungarian heralds began consequently to appear
in German towns, proclaiming aloud in street and
on market-place the words of their royal master.
Their voices found a ready echo among the people,
for this promised land was not absolutely unknown
to the German yeomen, who many of them had
passed through it on their way to and from the
Crusades : besides, this was the time when feudal
rights weighed most oppressively on unfortunate
vassals, and no doubt many were glad to purchase
freedom even at the price of expatriation.

As a German poet sings :—

> "When castles crowned each craggy height
>   Along the banks of Rhine,
> And 'neath the mailed warriors' might
>   Did simple burghers pine ;
>
> When bowed the common herd of men,
>   Serfs to a lord's commanding,—
> The holy Roman Empire then
>   For free men had no standing.
>
> Then off broke many and away,
>   Another country questing ;
> 'We'll found another home,' said they,
>   'A house on freedom resting.
>
> 'Hungarian forests, wild and free,
>   Are refuge for us keeping ;
> From home and home's dear ties will we
>   Emancipate us, weeping.' "

Or in the words of another :—

> " We'll ride away to the east,
> Away to the east we go—
>   O'er meadows away,
>   O'er meadows so gay ;
> It will be better so.
>
> And when we came to the east,
> 'Neath the lofty house came we,
>   They called us in,
>   O'er meadows so gay,
> And bade us welcome be."

In thus summoning German colonists to the country, the Hungarian monarch showed wisdom and policy far in advance of his century, as the result has proved. It was a bargain by which both parties were equally benefited, and thereby induced to keep the mutual compact. The Germans obtained freedom which they could not have had in their own country, while their presence was a guarantee to the monarch that this province would not be torn from his crown.

In the midst of a population of serfs, and side by side with proud and overbearing nobles, these German immigrants occupied a totally different and neutral position. Without being noble, they were free men every one of them, enjoying rights and privileges hitherto unknown in the country. Depending directly from the king, they had no other master, and were only obliged to go to war when the monarch in person commanded the expedition. For this reason the country inhabited by the Germans was often termed the Königs-boden, or Kingsland, and on their official seal were engraved the words, "Ad retinendam coronam."

Saxon Burgher in olden times.

The exact date of the arrival of these German colonists in Transylvania is unknown, but appears to have been between 1141 and 1161. That they did not all come at the same time is almost certain.

Probably they arrived in successive batches at different periods; for, as we see by history, all did not enjoy exactly the same privileges and rights, but different colonies had been formed under different conditions.

Also the question of what precise part of the German fatherland was the home of these out-wanderers is enveloped in some obscurity. They have retained no certain traditions to guide us to a conclusion, and German chronicles of that time make no mention of their departure. The Crusades, which at that epoch engrossed every mind, must have caused these emigrations to pass comparatively unnoticed. Only a sort of vague floating tradition is preserved to this day in some of the Transylvania villages, where on winter evenings some old grandam, shrivelled and bent, ensconced behind the blue-tiled stove, will relate to the listening bairns crowding around her knees how, many, many hundred years ago, their ancestors once dwelt on the sea-shore, near to the mouth of four rivers, which all flowed out of a yet larger and mightier river. In this shadowy description, probably the river Rhine may be recognised, the more so that in the year 1195 these German colonists are, in a yet existing document, alluded to as *Flanderers*. The name of *Sachsen* (Saxons), as they now call themselves, was only much later used as their general designation, and it is more than probable, from certain differences in language, customs, and features, that different colonies proceeded from widely different parts of the original mother-country.

Although the Hungarian kings generally kept their given word right nobly to the immigrants, yet these had much to suffer, both from Hungarian nobles jealous of the privileges they enjoyed, and from the older inhabitants of the soil, the Wallachians, who, living in a thoroughly barbaric state up in the mountains, used to make frequent raids down into the valleys and plains, there to pillage, burn, and murder whatever came into their hands. If we add to this the frequent invasions of Turks and Tartars, it seems a marvel how this little handful of Germans, brought into a strange country and surrounded by enemies on all sides, should have maintained their independence and preserved their identity under such combination of adverse circumstances. They built churches and fortresses, they formed schools and guilds, they made their own laws and elected their own judges; and in an age when Hungarian nobles could scarcely read or write, these little German colonies were so many havens of civilisation in the midst of a howling wilderness of ignorance and barbarism.

The German name of Transylvania — Siebenbürgen, or Seven-forts—was long supposed to have been derived from the seven principal fortresses erected at that time. Some recent historians are, however, of opinion that this name may be traced to *Cibinburg*, a fortress built near the river Cibin, from which the surrounding province, and finally the whole country, was called the land of the Cibinburg—of which, therefore, Siebenbürgen is merely a corruption.

Transylvania remained under the dependence of the Magyars till the year 1526, when, after the battle of Mohacs, which ended so disastrously for the Hungarians, Hungary was annexed to Austria, and Transylvania became an independent duchy, choosing its own regents, but paying, for the most part, a yearly tribute to Turkey.[1]

After something more than a century and a half of independence, Transylvania began to feel its position as an independent state to be an untenable one, and that its ultimate choice lay between

---

[1] The Turkish sway does not seem to have been a very oppressive one, if we are to believe this account of how the Turkish tax-surveyor used to collect his tithes :—

"In a cart harnessed with four horses, the Turkish tax-collector used to drive round the villages in Transylvania, and when he cracked his whip the people came running out and threw, each according to his means, a piece of money into the vat. Sometimes it was but a groat, sometimes even less, for there was but little money in the land at that time ; but the Turk was satisfied with what he got, and drove on without further ado."

complete subjection to either Turkey or Austria.
Making, therefore, a virtue of necessity, and hoping
thereby to escape the degradation of a conquered
province, Transylvania offered itself to Austria, and
was by special treaty enrolled in the Crown lands
of that empire in 1691.

Finally, in 1867, when the present emperor,
Francis Joseph, was crowned at Pesth, Transylvania
was once more formally united to Hungary, and,
like the rest of the kingdom, divided into *komitats*
or counties.

CHAPTER III.

POLITICAL.

IT is not possible, even in the most cursory account
of life and manners in Hungary, to escape all mention of the conflicting political interests which are
making of Austro-Hungary one of the most curious
ethnographical problems ever presented by history.
Taking even Transylvania alone, we should find
quite enough to fill a whole volume merely by
describing the respective relations of the different
races peopling the country. In addition to various
minor nationalities, we find here no less than three
principal races diametrically opposed to each other
in origin, language, habits, and religion—to wit, the
Magyars, the Saxons, and the Roumanians, whose
exact numbers I have given on a preceding page.
The gipsies, whose numbers figure next in the list
after the Saxons, need not here be taken into consideration, being absolutely devoid of all political
character; but of the other three races, each has its

individual aspirations and interests, and each a political object in view which it pursues with dogged persistency.

The Hungarians are at present the masters of the position, having wealth and nobility on their side, besides the reins of government. Since the year 1867, when Hungary, having regained her former independence with extended rights and privileges, re-established a purely Hungarian ministry and an independent Hungarian militia, the progress achieved in the country, both intellectually and commercially, has been remarkable, affording brilliant proof of what can be done by a handful of energetic and intelligent men against a vast majority of other races.

The total population of Hungary, rated at fifteen millions, counts four millions only of purely Hungarian individuals: the rest of the population is made up of Serbs, Croatians, Roumanians, Slovacks, and Germans, all of which (if we except the Germans, whose numbers are insignificant) are far inferior to the Magyars in point of civilisation; and here, as elsewhere, when intelligence and wealth are supported by energy, the right of might belonged to the Hungarians, who have always been able to produce skilful and efficient statesmen, knowing their own minds, and clear-sighted as to the country's requirements.

Those now at the helm have had the discernment from the very outset to foresee the danger likely to arise from the ever-increasing spirit of nationality gaining ground among the non-Hungarian inhabitants of the soil. Two courses were here open to them : either seeking to conciliate the various nationalities by concessions to their pretensions; or else, by pursuance of an inflexible policy, to sacrifice all alien considerations to purely Hungarian interests, and impose their own nationality on all without exception.

This latter course was the one adopted by Hungary, who for the last ten years, introducing measures as practical as they are far-sighted, has pursued this object with undeviating consistency.

First of all, the Hungarian tongue was everywhere established as the official language. In all schools, whether of Serbs, Roumanians, or Germans, it became compulsory to teach Hungarian; without a thorough knowledge of the language no one was competent to aspire to any official position; the courts of justice, even in completely non-Hungarian districts, are held in Hungarian, and Hungarian likewise is the word of command throughout the Honved army. Such are the means by which the Government hopes to effect the Magyarisation of all its subjects.

But within the last few years we have beheld

two new kingdoms spring up at Hungary's very door, Roumania and Serbia,—incentive enough to induce all Roumanians and Serbs living in Hungary strenuously to resist this Magyarising influence, and inspire them with the hope of being one day amalgamated with their more independent countrymen. In Croatia, the case is more or less the same, for, being united by similarities of language, custom, and religion to their Serbian neighbours, the Croats far rather incline to assimilate with these than with the tyrannical Magyars; while the Slovacks, continually stirred up by Russian, Ruthenian, and Bohemian agitators, have likewise their reasons for resistance. Add to this that the German colonies, which, far more isolated than the races afore-named, can never have a serious chance of independent existence, are yet infatuated enough to harbour impossible visions of a union with their fatherland, and have consequently ranged themselves among the most vehement opposers of Hungarian rule, and it will be seen that the task which the Magyars have set themselves, of bending all these conflicting interests to their own ends, is indeed a stupendous one. But Hungary, in self-preservation, could not have acted otherwise: it was for her a question of life or death; and having the choice of becoming the hammer or the anvil, who can blame her for choosing the former?

Whether this portentous struggle will outlast our generation, or find its issue within the next few years, will depend upon outward political constellations. So much, however, is certain, that should the Magyars be able to carry through their system during a sufficient space of time, they will have created a state which, by virtue of the richness of its soil, the extent of its domains, and the vigour of its race, will have acquired incontestable right to independent existence.

Should, however, the Oriental question, and with it the Panslavonian one, bring about the inevitable collision of nationalities so long foreseen; should the Balkan races begin to agitate ere Hungary have accomplished her herculean task,—then her downfall is certain. The Magyars may, indeed, continue to exist as a nation, but not as a state, and their fate will be that of Poland.

While in the one-half of the Austro-Hungarian empire this system of centralising the power and assimilating all minor interests to the Hungarian idea is being pursued with inflexible ardour, the Cis-Latin provinces—that is to say, Austria proper — are being governed in diametrically opposed fashion.

Till within a few years ago, the German language was the official one in all Cis-Latin provinces, and

Germans had there everywhere the upper hand, as to-day the Magyars in the Trans-Latin countries; but since the advent of Count Taafe's Ministry, now seven years ago, the situation has completely changed. The present Government, wishing to conciliate the different nationalities, such as Bohemians, Poles, Ruthenians, &c., granted to each of these the free use of its own tongue in school and office—a concession which may be said to mark the beginning of Austria's decomposition. The results of this deplorable system as yet have been, that the Germans, who in Austria form the wealthiest and most intelligent part of the population, embittered at finding themselves degraded from their former position of leaders of the state, have become the most formidable opponents of the Government; while the minor races, only stimulated by the concessions received, are ever clamouring for more. The Taafe Ministry has marvellously succeeded, during the incredibly short space of seven years, in establishing chaos in the administration of the Cis-Latin provinces, contenting no one, and fostering racial contentions which can have but the most melancholy results for the stability of the empire.

Whether a state, not only composed of such heterogeneous racial elements, but, moreover, govverned by two such diametrically opposed systems, will have strength to resist attacks from without, who can say?—for it still remains to be practically proved which of the two Governments has chosen the right road to success. So much, however, is certain—the Hungarians know what they want, and pursue their preconceived line of political action with consistent energy; while the Austrian Government, never knowing its own mind, is swayed at hazard by whichever of the minor nationalities happens to have the momentary ascendancy, and behindhand, as ever, of "an idea and of an army," may almost be said to deserve the definition of one of its own statesmen,[1] of being the "land of improbabilities."

[1] The late Count Beust.

CHAPTER IV.

THE War Office, whose ways are dark and whose mysteries are inscrutable, had unexpectedly decreed that we were to exchange Galicia for Transylvania.

The unaccountable decisions of a short-sighted Ministry, which, without ostensible reason, send unfortunate military families rolling about the empire like gigantic footballs—from Hungary to Poland, down to Croatia, and up again to Bohemia, all in one breath—too often burst on hapless German *ménages* like a devastating bomb, bringing moans and curses, tears and hysterics, in their train, according as the sufferer happens to be of choleric or lachrymose temperament. Only those who have lived in this country, and tasted of the bitter-sweets of Austrian military life, can tell how formidable it is to be forced to pack up everything —literally everything, from your stoutest kitchen-

chairs to your daintiest eggshell china—half-a-
dozen times during an equal number of years.

For my own part, however—and I am aware that
I am considered singular in my views—I had little
objection to being treated in this sportive fashion,
as long as it gave me the opportunity of seeing
fresh scenes and different types of people. There
are two sides to every question, a silver—or at
least a tinfoil—lining to every leaden cloud, and
it is surely wiser to regard one's self as a tourist
than as an exile?

What if crockery perish and mirrors be shivered
in the portentous flitting? Dry your eyes, and
console yourself by gazing at mountains new and
lakes unknown. And if furniture be annihilated,
and your grand pianoforte reduced to a wailing
discord, what of that? Such loss is only gain, for
in return you will hear the music of unknown
tongues and the murmur of strange waters. If
the proceeding be often illogical, the change is
always welcome; and on this particular occasion,
I secretly blessed the playful impetus which had
sent our ball of fate thus high up in the air, to
alight again in the land beyond the forest.

It was in the beginning of April that we started
on our journey, and in Galicia we left everything
still deep in ice and snow; but scarce had we passed
the Hungarian frontier, and got down on to the

broad plains, when a warm genial breeze came to
meet us and tell us that winter was gone. The
snow left us by degrees, and with it the poverty-
stricken careworn expression peculiar to Poland;
spring flowers ventured out of their hiding-places,
singly at first, then in groups of twos and threes,
till they grew to extensive patches of gold or
sapphire blue, pressing up to the rails on either side
of our way. Greasy *kaftans* began to give place
to sheepskin *bundas*, and pointed mustachios became more numerous than corkscrew ringlets.
The air seemed full of joyous music—the voice of
the lark and the strains of a gipsy fiddler alternately taking up the song of triumph over the return
of spring.

The railway communications are very badly
managed, so that it was only on the evening of the
second day (fully forty-eight hours) that we arrived
at Klausenburg, where we were to stop for a night's
rest. It would hardly have taken longer to go
from Lemberg to London.

Coming from the Hungarian plains, the entrance
into Transylvania is very striking, as the train
dashes along narrow winding valleys, where below,
a green mountain-torrent is breaking over grey
boulders—and above, the cliffs are piled up so high
and so near, that only by craning our necks out of
the carriage window can we catch a glimpse of the

sky above.   Unfortunately, the early darkness had
set in long before we reached Klausenburg, so that
I had no opportunity of observing the country
immediately round the town.

Fresh from Polish hotels as we were, the inn
where rooms had been secured struck us as well
kept and appointed, though I daresay that, had we
come from Vienna or Paris, it would have appeared
just fairly second-rate.   The beds were excellent,
the rooms clean; the doors could actually be locked
or bolted without superhuman effort; the bells
could really ring, and, what was stranger yet, their
summons was occasionally attended to.

I was somewhat disappointed next morning when
daylight came round again and showed me the
environs of the town.   Pretty enough, but tame and
insignificant, with nothing of the sublime grandeur
which the entrance into the land had led me to expect.   The town itself differed but little from many
other Hungarian towns I had seen before, and had
indeed an exclusively Hungarian character, being
the winter resort of the Magyar aristocracy of
Transylvania.

The present town of Klausenburg, or, in Hungarian, Koloszvar, lying 335 metres above the sea-
level, and built on the site of Napoca, a Roman
city, was founded by German colonists about the
year 1270-1272, and was for many years exclu-

sively a German town, where Hungarians were
only tolerated on sufferance and in one restricted
quarter. By degrees, however, these latter obtained a preponderance; and finally, when the
Unitarian sect made of Klausenburg its principal
seat, the Saxons withdrew in disgust from the
place altogether.

In the year 1658, Klausenburg was besieged by
the Tartars. The Turkish Sultan having deposed
George Rakoczy II. for acting against his will, sent
hither the barbarians to devastate the land. Burning and pillaging, the wild hordes reached Klausenburg (then a Saxon city), and standing before its
closed gates, they demanded a ransom of 30,000
thalers for sparing the town.

Martin Auer, the Klausenburg judge and a brave
Saxon man, went out to meet the enemy with a
portion of the required money. The Tartars threatened to murder him for not bringing the whole of
what they asked, but Auer divined that not even
the payment of the entire 30,000 thalers would
save the town from pillage. The Tartars intended
to take the sum, and then to sack the city. So he
begged to be suffered to go as far as the town-
gates in order to persuade his fellow-citizens to
deposit the rest of the money; but when he had
reached within speaking distance, he cried out to
his countrymen—

" Friends and citizens! I have come hither under
the feint of persuading you to pay the rest of the
fine demanded by the Tartars; but what I really
advise is for you to keep your money and resist
the enemy to the last: trust them not, for however much you pay, they will not spare you. For
my part, I gladly lay down my life for the good of
my people." But hardly had he finished speaking
when the Tartars, guessing at the purport of his
words, laid hold of the brave Saxon and dragged
him off to a cruel death.

A peculiar characteristic of Klausenburg are the
Unitarian divorces, which bring many strangers on
a flying visit to this town, where the conjugal knot
is untied with such pleasing alacrity, and replaced
at will by more congenial bonds.

To attain this end the divorcing party must be
a citizen of Klausenburg, and prove his possession
to house or land in the place. This, however, is
by no means so complicated as it sounds, the difficulty being provided for by a row of miserable
hovels chronically advertised for sale, and which
for a nominal price are continually passing from
hand to hand.

House-buying, divorce, and re-marriage can therefore be easily accomplished within a space of three
or four days—a very valuable arrangement for those
to whom time is money. By this convenient sys-

tem, therefore, if you happen to have quarrelled with your first wife on a Sunday, you have only to take the train to Klausenburg on Monday, become Unitarian on Tuesday, buy a house on Wednesday, be divorced on Thursday, re-married on Friday, and on Saturday sell your house and turn your back on the place with the new-chosen partner of your life, and likewise the pleasant *arrière-pensée* that you can begin again *da capo* next week if so pleases you.

I went to visit this street for sale, which presents a most doleful aspect. As the houses are continually changing hands, none of the transitory owners care to be at the expense of repairs or keeping in order; therefore rotten planking, hingeless gates, broken windows, and caved-in roofs are the general order of the day. A row of card-houses merely to mark this imaginary sort of proprietorship would equally fulfil the purpose.

The town is said to be unhealthy, and the mortality amongst children very great. This is attributed to the impurity of the drinking water, several of the springs which feed the town-wells running through the churchyard, which lies on a hill.

To our left, about an hour after leaving Klausenburg, we catch sight of the Thorda Cleft or *Spalt*, —one of the most remarkable natural phenomena which the county presents. It is nothing else but

The Thorda Spait.

[To face p. 34.

a gaping unexpected rift, of three or four English
miles in length, right through the limestone rocks,
which rise about 1200 feet at the highest point.
Deep and gloomy caverns, formerly the abode of
robbers, honeycomb these rocky walls, and a wild
mountain-torrent fills up the space between them,
completing a weirdly beautiful scene; but on our
first view of it from the railway-carriage it re-
sembled nothing so much as a magnified loaf of
bread severed in two by the cut of a gigantic knife.

I do not know how geologists account for the
formation of the Thorda Cleft, but the people explain it in their own fashion by a legend :—

The Hungarian King Ladislaus, surnamed the
Saint, defeated and pursued by his bitterest
enemies, the Kumanes, sought refuge in the mountains. He was already hard pressed for his life,
and close on his heels followed the pagans. Then,
in the greatest strait of need, with death staring
him in the face, the Christian monarch threw himself on his knees, praying to heaven for assistance.
And see! He forsaketh not those that trust in
Him! Suddenly the mountain is rent in twain,
and a deep yawning abyss divides the king from
his pursuers.

The rest of the country between Klausenburg
and Hermanstadt is bleak and uninteresting—it is,
in fact, as I afterwards learnt, one of the few ugly

stretches to be found in this land, of which it has so often been said that it is all beauty. A six hours' journey brought us to our destination, Hermanstadt, lying at the terminus of a small and sleepy branch railway. Unfortunately, with us also arrived the rain, streaming down in torrents, and blotting out all view of the landscape in a persistent and merciless manner; and for full eight days this dismal downpour kept steadily on, trying our patience and souring our tempers. What more exasperating situation can there be? To have come to a new place and yet be unable to see it: as soon be sent into an unknown picture-gallery with a bandage over the eyes.

There was, however, nothing to be done meanwhile but to dodge about the town under a dripping umbrella, and try to gain a general idea of its principal characteristics.

A little old-fashioned German town, sprited over here by supernatural agency; a town that has been sleeping for a hundred years, and is only now slowly and reluctantly waking up to life, yawning and stretching itself, and listening with incredulous wonder to the account of all that has happened in the outside world during its slumber,—such was the first impression I received of Hermanstadt. The top-heavy overhanging gables, the deserted watch-towers, the ancient ramparts, the crooked streets, in

whose midst the broad currents of a peaceful stream
partly fulfil the office of our newer-fashioned drains,
and where frequently the sprouting grass between
the irregular stone pavement would afford very fair
sustenance for a moderate flock of sheep, all com-
bine to give the impression of a past which has
scarcely gone and of a present which has not yet
penetrated.

There are curious old houses with closely grated
windows, whose iron bars are fancifully wrought
and twisted, sometimes in the shape of flowers and
branches, roses and briers interlaced, which seem
to have sprung up here to defend the chamber of
some beautiful princess lying spellbound in her
sleep of a hundred years. There are quaint little
gardens which one never succeeds in reaching, and
which in some inexplicable manner seem to be
built up in a third or fourth storey: sometimes in
spring we catch a glimpse of a burst of blossom
far overhead, or a wind-tossed rose will shower its
petals upon us, yet we cannot approach to gather
them. There is silence everywhere, save for occasional vague snatches of melody issuing from a
half-open window — old forgotten German tunes,
such as the " Mailüfterl " or " Anchen von Tharau,"
played on feeble, toneless spinnets. There are
nooks and corners and unexpected flights of steps
leading from the upper to the lower town, nar-

row passages and tunnels which connect opposite
streets.

"These are to enable the inhabitants to scuttle
away from the Turks," I was told, my informant
lowering his voice, as if we might expect a row of
turbans to appear at the other side of the passage
we were traversing. "There is our theatre," he
continued, pointing to a dumpy tower bulging out
of the rampart-wall. One of the principal strong-
holds this used to be ; but its shape now suited
conveniently for the erection of a stage, and the
narrow arrow-slits came in handy for the fixing up
of side-scenes.

Many more such old fortress-towers are to be
found all over the town, some of which are now
used as military stores, while others have been
converted into peaceable summer-houses. At the
time when Hermanstadt was still a Saxon strong-
hold each tower had its own name—as the Gold-
smith's Tower, the Tanner's, the Locksmith's, &c.,
according to the particular guild which manned it
in time of siege.

From one of these towers it was that the
Sultan Amurad was killed by an arrow when be-
sieging the town in 1438 with an army of 70,000
men.

The whole character of Hermanstadt is thoroughly old German, reminding me rather of some of the

Nuremberg streets or portions of Bregenz than of
anything to be seen in Hungary.

The streams which run down the centre of each
street are
no doubt as
enjoyable
for the ducks
who swim in
them, as for
young ladies
desirous of
displaying a
neat pair of
ankles; but
for more
hum-drum
mortals they
are some-
what of a
nuisance.
They can, it
is true, be
jumped in
dry weather

Old Fortress Tower on the ramparts at Hermanstadt.[1]

without particular danger to life or limb; but there
are many prejudiced persons who do not care to

[1] Reprinted from Publication of the Transylvanian Carpathian
Society.

transform a sober round of shopping into a species
of steeplechase, and who will persist in finding it
hard to be unable to purchase a yard of ribbon or a
packet of pins without taking several flying leaps
over swift watercourses.

Much of the life and occupations of our excellent
Saxon neighbours is betrayed by these tell-tale
streamlets, which, chameleon-like, alter their colour
according to what is going on around them.   Thus
on washing-days the rivulet in our street used to
be of a bright celestial blue, rivalling the laughing
Mediterranean in colour, unless indeed the family
in question were possessed of much scarlet hosiery
of inferior quality, in which case it would assume a
gory hue suggestive of secret murders.   When the
chimney-sweep had been paying his rounds in the
neighbourhood, the current would be dark and
gloomy as the turbid waters of the Styx; and
when a pig was killed a few doors off—— But
no; the subject threatens to grow too painful, and
I feel that a line must be drawn at the pig.

Such is the everyday aspect of affairs; but in
rainy weather these little brooklets, becoming ob-
streperous, swell out of all proportions, and for this
frequent contingency small transportable bridges
are kept in readiness to be placed across the
principal thoroughfares of the town.   After a
very heavy thunder-plump in summer, even these

bridges do not suffice, as then the whole street is flooded from side to side, and for an hour or so Hermanstadt becomes Venice—minus the gondolas.

These occasional floodings give rise to many amusing incidents, as that of an officer who, invited to dinner by the commanding general, beheld with dismay the dinner-hour approach. He had only to cross the street, or rather the canal, for at that moment it presented the appearance of a navigable river. Would the waves subside in time ? was his anxious question as he gazed at the clock in growing suspense, and dismally surveyed his beautifully fitting patent-leather boots. No, the waves did not subside, and no carriage was to be procured, the half-dozen *fiacres* of which Hermanstadt alone could boast being already engaged. The clock struck the quarter. " What is to be done ? " moaned the unhappy man in agony of spirit, while the desperate alternatives of swimming or of suicide began to dance before his fevered brain. " A boat, a boat, a kingdom for a boat ! " he repeated mechanically, when it struck him that the quotation might as well be taken literally in this case, and that in default of a boat, he had three good steeds in his stables. " Saddle my horse — my tallest one ! " he cried excitedly; " I am saved ! "— and so he was. The gallant steed bore him through the roaring flood, bringing him high and dry to the door of his host, with patent boots intact.

Meanwhile—to return to the subject of my first days at Hermanstadt—the rain had continued to fall for a whole week, and I was beginning to lose all patience. " I don't believe in the mountains you all tell me about!" I felt inclined to say, when my first eight days had shown me nothing but leaden clouds and dull grey mists; but even while I thought it, the clouds were rolling away, and bit by bit a splendid panorama was unfolding before my eyes.

Sure enough they were there, the mountains I had just been insulting by my disbelief, a long glittering row of snowy peaks shining in the out-bursting sunshine, so delicately transparent in their loveliness, so harmonious in their blended colour-ing, so sublimely grand in their sweeping lines, that I could have begged their pardon for having doubted their existence !

As one beautiful picture often suffices to light up a dingy apartment, so one lovely view gives life and interest to a monotonous county town. It takes the place of theatres, art galleries, and glit-tering shop-windows; it acts at times as a refresh-ing medicine or a stimulating tonic; and though I saw it daily, it used to strike me afresh with a

sense of delightful surprise whenever I stepped
round the corner of my street, and stood in face
of this glorious *tableau.*

The town of Hermanstadt lies in the centre of a
large and fertile plain, intersected by the serpentine curves of the river Cibin, and dotted over by
well-built Saxon villages. To the north and west
the land is but gently undulating, while to the east
and south the horizon is bounded by this imposing chain of the Fogarascher Hochgebirg, their
highest peaks but seldom free from snow, their
base streaked by alternate stretches of oak, beech,
and pine forests.

At one point this forest, which must formerly
have covered the entire plain, reaches still to the
farther end of the town, melting into the promenade, so that you can walk in the shade of
time-honoured oak-trees right to the foot of the
mountains—a distance of some eight English miles.

To complete my general sketch of the town of
Hermanstadt, I shall merely mention that although
our house was situated in one of the liveliest
streets, yet the passing through of a cart or carriage was a rare event, which, in its unwonted
excitement, instinctively caused every one to rush
to their windows; that the pointed irregular pavement, equally productive of corns and destructive
to *chaussure*, seems to be the remnant of some

medieval species of torture; that gas is unknown, and the town but insufficiently lighted by dingy petroleum lamps.

Probably by the time that Hermanstadt fully wakens up to life again, it will discover to its astonishment that it has slept through a whole era, and skipped the gas stage of existence altogether, for it will then be time to replace the antediluvian petroleum lamps, not by the already old-fashioned gas ones, but by the newer and more brilliant rays of electric light.

CHAPTER V.

As I happened to arrive at Hermanstadt[1] precisely
seven hundred years later than the German colonists who had founded that city, I had the good
luck to assist at a national festival of peculiarly
interesting character.

Of the town's foundation, old chronicles tell us
how the outwanderers, on reaching the large and
fertile plain where it now stands, drove two swords
crossways into the ground, and thereon took their
oath to be true and faithful subjects of the monarch who had called them hither, and with their
best heart's blood to defend the land which had
given them shelter. The two swords on which this
oath was registered were carefully preserved, and
sent, one to Broos and the other to Draas—two
towns marking the extremities of the Saxonland—

[1] The Hungarian name of Hermanstadt is Nagy-Szeben, and its
Roumanian appellation Sibiin.

there to be treasured up for ever. But in consequence of evil times which came over the land,
and of the war and bloodshed which devastated
it, one of these swords—that of Broos—got lost.
But we are told that the other is still to be seen
in the church of Draas. It is of man's length,
from which it is argued that these Saxon immigrants were well-grown and vigorous men.

Who this Herman was who gave his name to
the city can only be conjectured—probably one of
the leaders of the little band, for, as we see by the
names of some of the surrounding villages, each
has been called after some old German, whose
identity has not transpired, as Neppendorf from
Eppo, Hammersdorf from Humbert, &c., &c.

Some old chronicles, indeed, tell us that when
the Hungarian King Stephen I. was married to
Gisela, sister of the German King Henry II., there
came in her suite a poor Baron Herman, along
with his family, from Nuremberg to Transylvania,
and he it was who founded the settlement which
later developed into the present town of Hermanstadt. It is said that the first settlement was
formed in 1202; likewise that the said Herman
lived to the age of a hundred and twenty-five, and
was the progenitor of a renowned and powerful race.

Another legend accounts for the foundation of
Hermanstadt with the old well-worn tale which

has done duty for so many other cities, of a shepherd who, when allowed to take as much land as he could compass with a buffalo's hide, cut up the skin into narrow strips, and so contrived to secure a handsome property. This particular sharp-witted peasant was, by profession, a keeper of swine, and there is a fountain in the lower town which still goes by the name of the *funtine porcolor* or swineherd's well.

With all these conflicting statements staring one in the face, there did not seem to be (so far as I could learn) any very authentic reason for supposing Hermanstadt to have been founded precisely in 1184; but everybody had apparently made up their minds that such was the case, so the date was to be commemorated by a costumed procession, extensive preparations for which kept the quiet little town in a state of fermentation for many weeks beforehand.

All the tradesmen of the place seemed to have suddenly gone mad, and could hardly be induced to attend to the everyday wants of commonplace mortals whose ancestors had not the *prestige* of a seven-centuried expatriation. If I went to order a pair of walking-boots, I was disdainfully informed that I could not hope for them that week, as all hands were employed in fashioning high-peaked leather boots of yellow pig-skin for Herman and

his retainers. If I looked in at the glove-maker's
I fared no better, for he had lost all interest in pale
kids or *gants de suéde;* and the solitary pair of
Sarah Bernhardt gloves, hitherto the pride of his
show-window, had been ruthlessly cast aside to
make way for ponderous gauntlets of heroic dimensions. The tailors would have nothing to do
with vulgar coat or trousers, but had soared unani-
mously to the loftier regions of jerkins and galli-
gaskins; even the tinsmith had lost his mental
equilibrium, apparently labouring under the delusion that he was an ancient armourer who could
not possibly demean himself by mending a simple
modern pudding-mould.

We unfortunate strangers, bootless, gloveless,
coatless, and puddingless, as we were in those
days, had a very hard time of it indeed while
this national fever was at its height, and keenly
felt the terrible disadvantage of not having been
born as ancient Saxons. At last, however, the
preparations were complete, and forgetting our
privations, we were fain to acknowledge the sight
to be one of the most curious and exceptional we
had ever witnessed. The old-fashioned streets
made a fitting background for this medieval pageant, in which peasants and burghers, on foot and
on horseback; groups of maidens, quaintly attired,
plying the distaff as they went along; German

matrons, with jewelled head-dresses and cunningly wrought golden girdles; gaily ornamented chariots, bearing the fruits of the field or the trophies of the chase,—passed us in solemn procession; while on

Mounted Peasants from the Historical Procession.

a sylvan stage erected in the depths of the old oak forest, a simple but moving drama set forth the words and actions of the forefathers of those very actors—the German colonists who, seven hundred years previously, had come hither to seek a home in the wild Hungarian forests.

The costumes and procession had been arranged by native artists, and as a work of art, no doubt many parts of the performance were open to criticism. Some of our fashionable painters would assuredly have turned sick and faint at sight of the unfortunate combinations of colouring which frequently marred the effect of otherwise correctly arranged costumes. Whoever has lived in large towns must have seen such things better done, over and over again; but what gave this festival a unique stamp of originality, not to be attained by any amount of mere artistic arrangement, was the feeling which penetrated the whole scene and animated each single actor.

It is difficult to conceive, as it is impossible to describe, the deep and peculiar impression caused by this display of patriotism on the part of Germans who have never seen their fatherland — Rhinelanders who are not likely ever to behold the blue rushing waters of the Rhine. Until now we had always been taught that Germany was inhabited by Germans, France by Frenchmen, and England by Englishmen; but here we have such a complex medley of nationalities as wellnigh to upset all our schoolroom teaching. Listening to the words of the German drama, we can easily fancy ourselves at Cologne or Nuremberg, were it not for the dark faces of Roumanian peasants pushing forward to look at

the unwonted scene, and for the Hungarian uniforms of the *gendarmes* who are pushing them back.

More primitive but not less interesting than the
historical procession just described, is the way in
which the arrival of these German immigrants is
still yearly commemorated in the village of Nadesch.
There, on a particular day of the year, all the lads
dress up as pilgrims, in long woollen garments,
rope-girdles, and with massive staffs in their hands.
Thus attired, they assemble round the flag ; a venerable old man takes the lead, beating the drum ;
and, singing psalms, they go in procession down the
street, now and then entering some particularly
spacious courtyard, where a dance is executed and
refreshments partaken of. A visit to the pastor is
also *de rigueur*, and the procession only breaks up
at evenfall, after having traversed the whole village from end to end. When questioned as to
the signification of this custom, the people answer,
" Thus came our fathers, free people like ourselves,
from Saxonia into this land, behind the flag and
drum, and with staffs in their hands. And because
we have not ourselves invented this custom, neither
did our ancestors invent it, but have transmitted it
to us from generation to generation, so do we, too,
desire to hand it down to our children and grandchildren."

How these Germans came to settle so many hundred miles away from their own country has also formed the subject of numerous tales, none prettier nor more suggestive than their identification with the lost children of Hameln—a well-known German legend, rendered familiar to English readers through Browning's poem.

"It was in the year 1284" (so runs the tale) "that, in the little town of Hameln, in Westphalia, a strange individual made his appearance. He wore a coat of cloth of many colours, and announced himself as a rat-catcher, engaging to rid the town of all rats and mice for a certain sum of money. The bargain being struck, the rat-catcher drew out of his pocket a small pipe, and began whistling; whereupon from every barn, stable, cellar, and garret there issued forth a prodigious number of rats and mice, collecting in swarms round the stranger, all intent upon his music.

"All the vermin of the place being thus assembled, the piper, still playing, proceeded to the banks of the river Weser, and rolling up his breeches above the knee, he waded into the water, blindly followed by rats and mice, who were speedily drowned in the rushing current.

"But the burghers of Hameln, seeing themselves thus easily delivered from their plague, repented the heavy sum of money they had pro-

mised, putting off the payment, under various excuses, whenever the stranger claimed the reward
of his labours.

" At last the piper grew angry, and went away,
cursing the town which had behaved so dishonour-
ably; but he was seen to haunt the neighbourhood, dressed as a huntsman, with high-peaked
scarlet cap; and at daybreak on the 26th of June,
feast of St John, the shrill note of his pipe was
again heard in the streets of Hameln.

" This time neither rats nor mice responded to
the summons, for all vermin had perished in the
waters of the Weser; but the little children came
running out of the houses, struggling out of their
parents' arms, and could not be withheld from following the sinister piper.   In this way he led the
infantine procession to the foot of a neighbouring
hill, into which he disappeared along with the
children he had beguiled.   Among these was the
half-grown-up daughter of the burgomaster of
Hameln, a maiden of wondrous grace and beauty.

" A nursemaid, who, with a little one in her
arms, had been irresistibly compelled to join the
procession, found strength enough at the last moment to tear herself away, and, reaching the town
in breathless haste, brought the sad news to the
bereaved parents.   Also one little boy, who had
run out in his shirt, feeling cold, went back to

fetch his jacket, and was likewise saved from his comrades' fate ; for by the time he regained the hillside, the opening had closed up, leaving no trace of the mysterious piper nor of the hundred and thirty children who had followed him."

Nor were they ever found again by the heart-broken parents ; but popular tradition has averred the Germans who about that time made their appearance in Transylvania to be no other than the lost children of Hameln, who, having performed their long journey by subterranean passages, re-issued to the light of day through the opening of a cavern, known as the Almescher Höhle, in the north-east of Transylvania.

CHAPTER VI.

THE SAXONS : CHARACTER——EDUCATION——RELIGION.

WHOEVER has lived among these Transylvanian
Saxons, and has taken the trouble to study them,
must have remarked that not only seven centuries'
residence in a strange land and in midst of antagonistic races has made them lose none of their
identity, but that they are, so to say, *plus catholiques
que le pape*——that is, more thoroughly Teutonic than
the Germans living to-day in the original Fatherland. And it is just because of the adverse circumstances in which they were placed, and of the
opposition and attacks which met them on all sides,
that they have kept themselves so conservatively
unchanged. Feeling that every step in another
direction was a step towards the enemy, finding
that every concession they made threatened to become the link of a captive's chain, no wonder they
clung stubbornly, tenaciously, blindly to each pe-
culiarity of language, dress, and custom, in a man-

ner which has probably not got its parallel in
history. Left on their native soil and surrounded
by friends and countrymen, they would undoubtedly have changed as other nations have changed.
Their isolated position and the peculiar circumstances of their surroundings have kept them
what they were. Like a faithful portrait taken
in the prime of life, the picture still goes on showing the bloom of the cheek and the light of the
eye, long after time's destroying hand, withering
the original, has caused it to lose all resemblance to
its former self; and it is with something of the
feeling of gazing at such an old portrait that we
contemplate these German people who dress like
old bas-reliefs of the thirteenth and fourteenth
centuries, and continue to hoard up provisions
within the church walls, as in the days when besieged by Turk or Tartar. Such as these Saxons
wandered forth from the far west to seek a home
in a strange land, such we find them again to-day
seven centuries later, like a corpse frozen in a gla-
cier which comes to light unchanged after a long
lapse of years.

From an artistic point of view, these Saxons are
decidedly an unlovely race. There is a want of
flowing lines and curves and a superfluity of angles
about them, most distressing to a sensitive eye.
The women may usually be described as having

rather good hair, indifferent complexions, narrow shoulders, flat busts, and gigantic feet. Their features, of a sadly unfinished wooden appearance, irresistibly reminded me of the figures of Noah and his family out of a sixpenny Noah's ark. There is something Noah's-ark-like, too, about their attire, which, running entirely in hard straight lines, with nothing graceful or flowing about them, no doubt helped to produce this Scriptural impression. The Saxon peasant is stiff without dignity, just as he is honest without being frank. Were the whole world peopled by this race alone, our dictionaries might have been lightened of a good many unnecessary words, such as elegance, grace, fascination, &c.

Of course now and then one comes across an exception to this general rule, and finds a pretty girl, like a white poppy in a field of red ones; but such exceptions are few and far between, and I have remarked that on an average it takes three well-populated villages to produce two bonnie lassies.

The men are on the whole pleasanter to look at than the fair sex, having often a certain ungainly picturesqueness of their own, reminding one of old Flemish paintings.

Something hard and grasping, avaricious and mistrustful, characterises the expression of most

Saxon peasants. For this, however, they are scarcely to blame, any more than for their flat busts and large feet—their character, and consequently their expression, being but the natural result of circumstances, the upshot of seven centuries of stubborn resistance and warfare with those around them. "We Saxons have always been cheated or betrayed whenever we have had to do with strangers," they say; and no doubt they are right. The habit of mistrust developed almost to an instinct cannot be easily got rid of, even if there be no longer cause to justify it.

This defensive attitude towards strangers which pervades the Saxons' every word and action, makes it, however, difficult to feel prepossessed in their favour. Taken in the sense of antiquities, they are no doubt an extremely interesting people, but viewed as living men and women, not at first sight attractive to a stranger; and while compelling our admiration by the solid virtues and independent spirit which have kept him what he is, the Saxon peasant often shows to disadvantage beside his less civilised, less educated, and also less honest neighbour, the Roumanian.

As a natural consequence of this mistrust, the spirit of speculation is here but little developed—for speculation cannot exist without some degree of confidence in one's neighbour. They do not care to risk one florin in order to gain ten, but are content to keep a firm grasp on what they have got. There are no beggars at all to be seen in Saxon towns, and one never hears of large fortunes gained or lost. Those who happen to be wealthy have only become so by the simple but somewhat tedious process of spending half their income only, during a period of half a century; and after they have in this manner achieved wealth, it does not seem to profit them much, for they go on living as they did before, nourishing themselves on scanty fare, and going to bed early in order to save the expense of lights.

The town folk are weaker and punier editions of the villagers, frequently showing marks of a race degenerated from constant intermarriage; and, stripped of their ancient Noah's-ark costume, lose much of their attraction.

They are essentially a *bourgeois* nation, possessing neither titles nor nobility of their own, although many can boast of lengthy pedigrees. Those who happen to be *Adel* (noble) have only obtained their *von* in some exceptional manner in later times, and the five-pointed crown seems somewhat of an anomaly.

Although the Saxons talk of Germany as their Fatherland, yet their patriotic feeling is by no means what we are accustomed to understand by that word. Their attachment to the old country would seem rather to be of prosaic than romantic sort. " We attach ourselves to the German nation and language," they say, endeavouring to explain the complicated nature of their patriotism, " because it offers us the greatest advantages of civilisation and culture : we should equally have attached ourselves to any other nation which offered us equal advantages, whether that nation had happened to be Hungarian, French, or Chinese. If the Hungarians had happened to be more civilised than ourselves, we should have been amalgamated with them long ago." [1]

Such an incomprehensible sort of patriot would probably have been condemned by Scott to go down to his grave " unwept, unhonoured, and unsung." But I suppose that allowances must be made for their peculiar position, and that it is difficult to realise what it feels like to be á grafted plant.

There is one village in Transylvania which, isolated in the midst of a Hungarian population, offers an instance of a more complex species of nationality than any I have yet heard of. This is the village of Szass Lona, near Klausenburg, which used to be Saxon, but where the people have gradually forgot-

[1] This, however, may be doubted, as I do not believe that, under any circumstances, a natural amalgamation between Germans and Magyars could ever have come about. There is a too deeply inrooted dislike between the two races.

ten their own mother-tongue, and can only speak Hungarian. There is, however, no drop of Hungarian blood in their veins, as they marry exclusively amongst themselves, and they have retained alike the German type of feature and the national Saxon dress intact in all its characteristics. Also the family names throughout the village are German ones—as Hindrik, Tod, Jäger, Hubert, &c.

Though none of these people can speak a word of German, and no one can remember the time when German was spoken in the village, yet during the revolution of 1848 these Hungarian-speaking Germans rose to a man to fight against the Magyars.

The Saxon dialect—totally distinct from modern German—has, I am told, most resemblance to the *patois* spoken by the peasants near Luxemburg. It is harsh and unpleasant to the ear, but has in some far-off and indefinable way a certain caricatured likeness to English. Often have I been surprised into turning round sharply in the street to see who could be speaking English behind me, only to discover two Saxon peasants comparing notes as to the result of their marketing.

The language, however, differs considerably in different neighbourhoods; and a story is told of natives of two different Saxon villages, who, being unable to understand each other, were reduced to conversing in Roumanian.

The *Sachsengraf* (Count), or Comes, was formerly the head of the nation, chosen by the people, and acknowledging no other authority but that of the king.   He was at once the judge and the leader of his people, and had alone the power of pronouncing sentence of death, in token of which four fir-trees were planted in front of his house.   The original meaning of this I take to be, that in olden times the malefactors were executed on the spot and suspended on these very trees, in full sight of the windows—a pleasant sight, truly, for the ladies of the family.

Nowadays the Saxon Comes has shrunk to a mere shadow of his former self; for though there is still nominally a Comes who resides at Herman-stadt, his position is as unlike what it used to be as those four trumpery-looking little Christmas-trees stuck before his door resemble the portentous gallows of which they are the emblem.   It is, in fact, merely as a harmless concession to Saxon national feeling that the title has been preserved at all—a mere meaningless appendage tacked on to the person of the Hungarian *Obergespan*, or sheriff.

The principal strength of these Saxon colonists has always lain in their schools, whose conservation they jealously guard, supporting them entirely from their own resources, and stubbornly refusing all help from Government. They do not wish to accept favours, they say, and thereby incur obligations. These schools had formerly the name of being among the very best in Austria; and I have heard of many people who from a distance used to send their children to study there, some twenty to thirty years ago. That this reputation is, however, highly overrated is an undoubted fact, as I know from sad experience with my own children, though it is not easy to determine where the fault exactly lies. The Saxons declare their schools to have suffered from Hungarian interference, which limits their programme in some respects, while insisting on the Hungarian language being taught in every class; but many people consider the Saxons themselves quite as much to blame for the bad results of their teaching. Doubtless in this as in other respects, it is their exaggerated conservatism which is at fault; and, keeping no account of the age we live in, what was reckoned good some thirty years ago may be called bad to-day.

Anyhow, between the reforming Hungarians and the conservative Saxons, unfortunate stranger boys have a very hard time of it indeed at the Hermanstadt Gymnasium, and it is a fact beginning to be generally acknowledged that children coming to Austria from Transylvanian schools are thrown two whole classes back.

But the whole question of education in Austria is such a provoking and unsatisfactory one, that it is hardly possible to speak of it with either patience or politeness; and by none are its evil effects more disastrously felt than by hapless military families, who, compelled to shift about in restless fashion from land to land, are alternately obliged to conform their children to the most opposite requirements of utterly different systems.

Thus the son of an officer serving in the Austrian army may be obliged to study half-a-dozen different languages (in addition to Latin, Greek, German, and French) during a hardly greater number of years. He must learn Italian because his father is serving at Trieste, and may be getting on fairly well with that language when he is abruptly called upon to change it for Polish, since Cracow is henceforth the town where he is to pursue his studies. But hardly has he got familiar with the soft Slave tongue, when, ten to one, his accent will be ruined for life by an untimely transition to Bohemia, where the hideous Czech language has become *de rigueur*. Slavonian and Ruthenian may very likely have their turn at the unfortunate infant before he has attained the age of twelve, unless the distracted father be reduced to sacrifice his military career to the education of his son.

It is not of our own individual case that I would

speak thus strongly, for our boys being only burdened with seven languages (to wit, Polish, English, German, French, Greek, Latin, and Hungarian),
would scarcely be counted ill-used, as Austrian
boys go, having escaped Bohemian, Slavonian,
Ruthenian, and Italian; yet assuredly to us it was
a very happy day indeed when we made a bonfire
of the Magyar school-books, and ceased quaking
at sight of the formidable individual who taught
Hungarian at the Hermanstadt Gymnasium.

O happy English schoolboys, you know not
how much you have to be thankful for!—your own
noble language, adorned with a superficial layer of
Greek and Latin, and at most supplemented by a
little atrocious French, being sufficient to set you
up for life. Think of those others who are pining
in a complicated network of Bohemian, Polish,
Hungarian, Slavonian, Italian, Croatian, and Ruthenian fetters; think of them, and drop a sym-
pathising tear over their mournful lot!

That the Saxon school-professors are well-edu-
cated, intelligent men, is no proof in favour of the
schools themselves, for here another motive is at
work. No man can, namely, aspire to be pastor
without passing through the university, and then
practising for several years at a public gymnasium;
and as these places are very lucrative, there is a
great run upon them. Now, as formerly, most

young men are sent to complete their studies at
some German university town—Heidelberg, Göt-
tingen, or Jena—an undertaking which, before the
days of railroads, must have required considerable
resolution to enable those concerned to encounter
the hardships of a journey which took from ten to
twelve weeks to perform. It was usually conducted
in the following manner: Some enterprising Roumanian peasant harnessed twelve to fourteen horses
to some lumbering vehicle, and, laden with a dozen
or more students thirsting for knowledge, pilgered
thus to the German university town some eight or
nine hundred miles off. Returning to Transylvania some six months later, he brought back another batch of young men who had completed their
studies.

The weight which these Saxons have always attached to education may be gathered from the fact
that in almost each of their fortified churches or
Burgs there was a tower set apart for the inculca-
tion of knowledge, and to this day many such are
still in existence, and known as the *Schul thurm*
(school tower). Even when the enemy was standing outside the walls, the course of learning was
not allowed to be interrupted. It must have been
a strange sight and a worthy subject for some historical painter to see this crowd of old-fashioned
fair-haired children, all huddled together within

the dingy turret; some of the bolder or more inquisitive flaxen heads peering out of the narrow gullet windows at the turbans and crescents below, while the grim-faced mentor, stick in hand, recalls them to order, vainly endeavouring to fix their wandering attention each time a paynim arrow whizzed past the opening.

Why these Saxons, who have shown themselves so rigidly conservative on all other points, should nevertheless have changed their religion, might puzzle a stranger at first sight. The mere spirit of imitation would not seem sufficient to account for it, and Luther's voice could hardly have penetrated to this out-of-the-way corner of Europe at a time when telegraphs and telephones were yet unknown. The solution of this riddle is, however, quite simple, and lies close at hand, when we remember that even before the Reformation all those preparing for the Sacerdoce went to Germany to complete their studies. These, consequently, caught the reforming infection, and brought it back fresh from headquarters, acting, in fact, as so many living telephones, who, conveying the great reformer's voice from one end of Europe to the other, promulgated his doctrines with all the enthusiasm and fire of youth.

Every year thus brought fresh recruits from the

scene of action : no wonder then that the original Catholic clerical party grew daily smaller and
weaker, and proved unable to stem this powerful
new current. The contest was necessarily an unequal one: on one side, impassioned rhetoric and the
fire of youth ; on the other, the drowsy resistance
of a handful of superannuated men, grown rusty in
their theology and lax in the exercise of their duties.

In the year 1523, Luther's teaching had already
struck such firm roots at Hermanstadt, that the
Archbishop of Gran, to whose diocese Hermanstadt
then belonged, obtained a royal decree authorising
the destruction of all Lutheran books and documents, as pernicious and heretical. Accordingly an
archiepiscopal commissary was despatched to Hermanstadt, and all burghers were compelled to deliver up their Protestant books and writings to be
burnt in the public market-place. It is related
that on this occasion, when the bonfire was at its
highest, the wind, seizing hold of a semi-consumed
psalter, carried it with such force against the head
of the bishop's emissary, that, severely burnt, he
fainted away on the spot. The book was thrown
back into the fire, where it soon burned to ashes,
but the commissary died of the wounds received
the third day after the accident.

Another anecdote relating to the Reformation is
told of the village of Schass, which, while Luther's

doctrine was being spread in Transylvania, despatched one of its parishioners, named Strell, to
Rome in quest of a Papal indulgence for the community. More than once already had Strell been
sent to Rome on a like errand, and each time, on
returning home with the granted indulgence for his
people, he was received by a solemn procession of
all the villagers, bearing flying banners and singing
sacred hymns. He was, therefore, not a little surprised this time, on approaching the village, to see
the road deserted before him, though he had given
warning of his intended arrival. The bells were
dumb, and not a soul came out to meet him; but
his astonishment reached its climax when, on near-
ing the church, he perceived the images of the
saints he had been wont to revere lying in the mire
outside the church walls. To his wondering question he received the reply that in his absence the
villagers had changed their faith. Strell, however,
did not imitate their example, but raising up the
holy images from their inglorious position, he gave
them an honourable place in his house, remaining
Catholic to the end of his days.

Nevertheless, in spite of many such incidents,
the change of religion in Transylvania brought
about fewer disturbances than in most other places.
There was little strife or bloodshed, and none of
that fierce fanaticism which has so often injured

and weakened both causes. The Saxon peasantry did this as they do everything else, calmly and practically; and the Government permitting each party to follow its own religion unmolested, in a comparatively short time peace and order were re-established in the interior of the country.

Without wishing to touch on such a very serious subject as the respective merits of the two religions, or attempting to obtrude personal convictions, it seems to me, from a purely artistic point of view, that the sterner and simpler Protestant religion fits these independent and puritanical-looking Saxon folk far better than the ancient faith can have done; while the more graceful forms of the Oriental Church, its mystic ceremonies and arbitrary doctrines, are unquestionably better adapted to an ardent, ignorant, and superstitious race like the Roumanian one.

CHAPTER VII.

SAXON VILLAGES.

SAXON villages are easily distinguished from Roumanian ones, composed of wretched earthen hovels, as from Hungarian hamlets, which are marked by a sort of formal simplicity. The Saxon houses are larger and more massive; each one, solidly built of stone, stands within a roomy courtyard surrounded by a formidable stone wall. Building and repairing is the Saxon peasant's favourite employment, and the Hungarian says of him ironically, that when the German has nothing better to do, he pulls down his house and builds it up again by way of amusement.

Each village is usually formed of one long principal street, extending sometimes fully an English mile along the highroad. Only when the village happens to be built at a junction of several roads, the streets form a cross or triangle, in the centre of which mostly stands the church.

From this principal street or streets there some-times branch off smaller by-streets on either side ; but these are seldom more than five or six houses deep, for the Saxon lays great stress on the point of locality, and the question of high-street or by-street is to him every whit as important as the alternative of Grosvenor Square or City would be to a Londoner.

Formerly no Roumanians nor gipsies were toler-ated within Saxon villages, but of late these people have been gradually creeping nearer, and now most German villages have at one end a shabby sort of *faubourg* or suburb, composed of Roumanian and gipsy hovels.

The principal street, often broad enough to admit of eight carts driving abreast, presents but little life at first sight. The windows of the broad gable-end next the street have often got their shutters closed, for this is the best room, reserved for state occasions. Only when we open the gate and step into the large courtyard can we gain some insight into the life and occupations of the inhabitants.

Near to the entrance stands the deep draw-well, and all round are built the sheds and stables for sheep, horses, cows, and buffaloes, while behind these buildings another gate generally opens into a spacious kitchen-garden. From the court five or six steps lead up to a sort of open verandah, where the peasant can sit in summer and overlook his farm labourers. From this passage is entered the kitchen, to the right and left of which are respectively the common and the best room, both good-sized apartments, with two windows each. In

Saxon Peasant House.

addition to these, there is often a smaller one-windowed room, in which reside a young married couple, son or daughter of the house, who have not yet had time to found their own hearth-stone; or else there lives here the old widowed father or mother, who has abdicated in favour of the young people. A ladder or rough flight of steps leads to

the loft, and below the verandah is the entrance
to the cellar, where stores of pickled *Sauerkraut*,
the dearly beloved national dish of the Saxons, and casks of their pearly amber-coloured
wine, are among the principal features of the
provisions.

In the village street, in front of each peasant
house, there used formerly to stand a large fruit-
tree—pear, apple, or sometimes mulberry—whose
spreading branches cast a pleasant shade over the
stone bench placed there for the convenience of
those who like to enjoy a "crack" with the neighbours on fine evenings after the work is done.
Many of these trees have now been cut down, for
it was found that the godless gipsies used to make
their harvest there while the pious Saxons were at
church; or else unmannerly school-urchins in pelt-
ing down the fruit with stones would sometimes
hit the window-panes instead, and thus cause still
greater damage. The result is, therefore, that most
Saxon villages now present a somewhat bleak and
staring appearance, and that on a burning summer
day it is not easy to find a shady bench on which
to rest awhile.

It may be of interest here to quote the statistical
figures relating to a large and flourishing village in
the north-east of Transylvania :—

Houses, 326 (of these 32 are earth hovels).

Heads of population, 1416—of these the proportion of different nationalities as follows :—

Saxons—481 male, 499 female.
Hungarians—2.
Roumanians—118 male, 83 female (mostly farm-servants).
Tziganes—104 men, 106 women.
Jews—14 male, 9 female.

In this village, which is exceptionally rich in cattle, the different animals number :—

Bulls,	.	.	3	Horses,	.	.	475
Cows,	.	.	357	Goats,	.	.	182
Young cattle,		.	575	Pigs,	.	.	734
Oxen,	.	.	1200	Sheep,	.	1000-1500
Buffaloes,	.	.	120				

Most of the sheep in Transylvania are in the hands of the Roumanians, while the pigs invariably belong to the Saxons. Amongst these latter, 1000 men possess on an average 215 horses, while among the Szekels only 51 will be found to the same number of heads.

The Saxon peasant, being an enemy to all modern improvements, goes on cultivating his fields much as did his forefathers 600 years ago. Clinging to the antiquated superstition that a field is the more productive the longer it lies fallow, each piece of ground is ploughed and sowed once only in three years; and having, owing to the insufficient population, rarely enough hands to till his land himself, he is obliged to call in the assistance of Roumanian farm-servants.

Other people, too, have taken advantage of this agricultural somnolency of the Saxons : so the Bulgarians who pilger hither in troops every spring-time to rent the Saxons' superfluous fields, bringing with them their own tools and seed, and in autumn, having realised the profit of their labour, wend back their way to their homes and families. The great speciality of these Bulgarian farmers is onions, of which they contrive to rear vast crops far superior in size and quality to those grown by the natives. A Bulgarian onion-field is easily distinguished from a Saxon one by its trim orderly appearance, the perfect regularity with which the rows are planted, and the ingenious arrangements for providing water in time of drought.

Of the numerous Saxon villages which dot the plain around Hermanstadt, I shall only here attempt to mention two or three of those with which I have the most intimate acquaintance, as having formed the object of many a walk and ride. First, there is Heltau—which, however, has rather the character of a market-town than a village—lying in a deep hollow at the foot of the hills south of Hermanstadt, and with nothing either rural or picturesque about it. Yet whoever chances first to behold Heltau, as I did, on a fine evening in May when the fruit-trees are in full blossom, will carry

OLD TOWN GATE AT HERMANSTADT.

ON THE HELTAN SIDE.

PHOTOGRAPHED BY MADAME KAMILLA ASBOTH, HERMANSTADT

away an impression not easily forgotten. From
the road, which leads down in serpentine curves,
the village bursts on our eyes literally framed in
a thick garland of blossom, snowy white and delicate peach colour combining to cast a fictitious
glamour over what is in reality a very unattractive
place.

The inhabitants of Heltau, nearly all cloth-
makers by trade, fabricate that rough white cloth,
somewhat akin to flannel, of which the Roumanians' hose is made. It is also largely exported
to different parts of the empire, and Polish Jews
are often seen to hover about the place. Such,
in fact, is the attraction exercised by this white
woollen tissue, that a colony of the children of
Israel would have been formed here long ago,
had not the wary Saxons strenuously opposed such
encroachment.

Once riding past here in autumn, I was puzzled
to remark several whole fields near Heltau bearing
a white appearance almost like that of snow, yet
scarcely white enough for that : on coming nearer,
this whiteness resolved itself into wool, vast quantities of which, covering several acres of ground,
had been put out there to dry after the triple
washing necessary to render it fit for weaving
purposes.

The church at Heltau rejoices in the distinction

of four turrets affixed to the belfry-tower, which turrets were at one time the cause of much dissension between Heltau and Hermanstadt. It was not allowed for any village church to indulge in such luxuries—four turrets being a mark of civic authority only accorded to towns; but in 1590, when the church at Heltau was burnt down, the villagers built it up again as it now stands—a piece of presumption which Hermanstadt at first refused to sanction. The matter was finally compromised by the Heltauers consenting to sign a document, wherein they declared the four turrets to have been put there merely in guise of ornamentation, giving them no additional privileges whatsoever, and that they pledged themselves to remain as before submissive to the authority of Hermanstadt.

Some people, however, allege Heltau, or, as it used to be called, "The Helt," to be of more ancient origin than Hermanstadt—concluding from the fact that formerly the shoemakers, hatters, and other tradesmen here resided, but that during the pest all the inhabitants dying out to the number of seven, the land around was suffered to fall into neglect. Then the emperor sent other Germans to repeople the town, and the burghers of Hermanstadt came and bought up the privileges of the Heltauers.

The excellence of the Heltau pickled *Sauerkraut* is celebrated in a Saxon rhyme, which runs somewhat as follows :—

> " Draaser wheaten bread,
> Heltau's cabbage red,
> Streitford's bacon fine,
> Bolkatsch pearly wine,
> Schässburg's maidens fair,
> Goodly things and rare."

But more celebrated still is Heltau because of the unusually high stature of its natives, which an illnatured story has tried to account for by the fact of a detachment of grenadiers having been here quartered for several years towards the end of last century.

To the west of Heltau, nestling up close to the hills, lies the smaller but far more picturesque village of Michelsberg, one of the few Saxon villages which have as yet resisted all attempts from Roumanians or gipsies to graft themselves on to their community. Michelsberg is specially remarkable because of the ruined church which, surrounded by fortified walls, is situated on a steep conical mound rising some two hundred feet above the village. The church itself, though not much to look at, boasts of a Romanesque portal of singular beauty, which many people come hither to see. The original fortress which stood on this spot is said to have been built by a noble knight, Michel

of Nuremberg, who came into the country at the
same time that came Herman, who founded Hermanstadt.   Michel brought with him twenty-six
squires, and with them raised the fortress; but
soon after its completion he and his followers got
dispersed over the land, and were heard of no more.

Michelsberg.

The fortress then became the property of the villagers, who later erected a church on its site.

The Michelsbergers make baskets and straw hats,
and lately, wood-carving has begun to be developed as a native industry.   They have also the
reputation—I know not with what foundation—
of being bird-stealers; and I believe nothing will
put a Michelsberger into such a rage as to imitate
the bird-call used to decoy blackbirds and nightin-

gales to their ruin. This he takes to be an insulting allusion to his supposed profession.

In the hot summer months, many of the Hermanstadt burghers come out to Michelsberg for change of air and coolness, and we ourselves spent some weeks right pleasantly in one of the peasant houses which, consisting of two rooms and a kitchen, are let to visitors for the season. But it was strange to learn that this remote mountain-village is the self-chosen exile of a modern recluse —a well-born Hanoverian gentleman, Baron K——, who for the last half-dozen years has lived here summer and winter. Neither very old nor yet very young, he lives a solitary life, avoiding acquaintances; and though I lived here fully a month, I only succeeded in catching a distant glimpse of him.

Midsummer idleness being usually productive of all sorts of idle thoughts and fancies, we could not refrain from speculating on the reasons which were powerful enough thus to cause an educated man to bury himself alive so many hundred miles away from his own country in an obscure mountain-village; and unknown to himself, the mysterious baron became the hero of a whole series of fantastic air-castles, in which he alternately figured as a species of Napoleon, Diogenes, Eugene Aram, or Abälard. Whichever he was, however—and it

certainly is no business of mine—I can well ima-
gine the idyllic surroundings of Michelsberg to be
peculiarly fit to soothe a ruffled or wounded spirit.
Wrecked ambition or disappointed love must lose
much of their bitterness in this secluded nook, so
far removed from the echoes of a turbulent world.

Another village deserving a word of notice is
Hammersdorf, lying north of Hermanstadt—a pleasant walk through the fields of little more than
half an hour. The village, built up against gently
undulating hills covered with vineyards, is mentioned in the year 1309 as Villa Humperti, and is
believed to stand on the site of an old Roman
settlement. Scarcely a year passes without Roman
coins or other antiquities being found in the soil.

From the top of the Grigori-Berg, which rises
some 1800 feet directly behind the village, a very
extensive view may be enjoyed of the plains about
Hermanstadt, and the imposing chain of the For-
garascher mountains straight opposite.

Hammersdorf is considered to be a peculiarly
aristocratic village, and its inhabitants, who pride
themselves on being the richest peasants in those
parts, and on their womankind possessing the finest
clothes and the most valuable ornaments, are called
arrogant and stuck-up by other communities.

It is usual for the name of the house-owner and the

date of building to be painted outside each house;
but there are differences to be remarked in each
place—slight variations in building and decoration,
as well as in manner, dress, and speech of the
natives, spite of the general resemblance all bear
to each other.

Some houses have got pretty designs of conventional flowers painted in black or in contrasting
colour on their gable ends, and in many villages
it is usual to have some motto or sentence inscribed on each house. These are frequently of a
religious character, often a text from the Bible or
some stereotyped moral sentiment. Occasionally,
however, we come across inscriptions of greater
originality, which seem to be a reflection of the
particular individual whose house they adorn, as,
for instance, the following :—

> " I do not care to brag or boast,
>   I speak the truth to all,
> And whosoever does not wish
>   Myself his friend to call,
> Why then he's free to paint himself
>   A better on the wall."

Or else this sentence, inscribed on a straw-thatched
cottage :—

> " Till money I get from my father-in-law,
>   My roof it, alas ! must be covered with straw."

While the following one instantaneously suggests

the portrait of some stolid-faced, sleepy individual whose ambition has never soared beyond the confines of his turnip-field, or the roof of his pigsty :—

> " Too much thinking weakens ever—
>   Think not, then, in verse nor prose,
> For return the past will never,
>   And the future no man knows."

Many of the favourite maxims refer to the end of man, and give a somewhat gloomy colouring to a street when several of this sort are found in succession :—

> " Man is like a fragile flower,
>   Only blooming for an hour;
> Fresh to-day and rosy-red,
>   But to-morrow cold and dead."

Or else—

> " Within this house a guest to-day,
>   So long the Lord doth let me live;
> But when He bids, I must away—
>   Against His will I cannot strive."

Here another—

> " If I from my door go out,
>   Death for me doth wait without;
> And if in my house I stay,
>   He will come for me some day."

The mistrustful character of the Saxon finds vent in many inscriptions, of which I give a few specimens :—

> " Trust yourself to only one—
>   'Tis not wise to trust to none;
> Better, though, to have no friend
>   Than on many to depend."

" If you have a secret got,
  To a woman tell it not;
  For my part, I would as lieve
  Keep the water in a sieve."

" When I have both gold and wine,
  Many men are brothers mine;
  When the money it is done,
  And the wine has ceased to run,
  Then the brothers, too, are gone."

" Hardly do a man I see
  But who hates and envies me;
  Inside them their heart doth burn
  For to do an evil turn,
  Grudge me sore my daily bread;
  More than one doth wish me dead."

" Those who build on the highway,
  Must not heed what gossips say."

The four last I here give are among the best I
have come across, the first of these having a slightly
Shakespearian flavour about it :—

" Tell me for what gold is fit?
  Who has got none, longs for it;
  Who has got it, fears for thieves;
  Who has lost it, ever grieves."

" We cannot always dance and sing,
    Nor can each day be fair,
  Nor could we live if every day
    Were dark with grief and care;
  But fair and dark days, turn about,
    This we right well can bear."

" Say who is to pay now the tax to the king?
  For priests and officials will do no such thing;
  The nobleman haughty will pay nought, I vouch,
  And poor is the beggar, and empty his pouch;

The peasant alone he toileth to give
The means to enable those others to live."

" How to content every man,
    Is a trick which no one can ;
    If to do so you can claim,
    Rub this out and write your name."

Among the many house-inscriptions I have seen
in Transylvania, I have never come across any re-
ferring to love or conjugal happiness. The well-
known lines of Schiller—

" Raum ist in der kleinsten Hütte
    Für ein glücklich liebend Paar," [1]—

of which one gets such a surfeit in Germany, are
here conspicuous by their absence. This will not
surprise any one acquainted with the domestic life
of these people. Any such sentiment would most
likely have lost its signification long before the
wind and the rain had effaced it, for it would not
at all suit the Saxon peasant to change his house-
motto as often as he does his wife.

[1] " There is space in the smallest hut
    To contain a happy loving couple."

CHAPTER VIII.

SAXON INTERIORS—CHARACTER.

THE old china mania, which I hear is beginning to die out in England, has only lately become epidemic in Austria; and as I, like many others, have been slightly touched by this malady, the quaintly decorated pottery wine-jugs still to be found in many Saxon peasant houses offered a new and interesting field of research.

These jugs are by no means so plentiful nor so cheap as they were a few years ago, for cunning *bric-a-brac* Jews have found out this hitherto unknown store of antiquities, and pilger hither from the capital to buy up wholesale whatever they find. Yet by a little patience and perseverance, any one living in the country may yet find enough old curiosities to satisfy a reasonable mania; and while seeking for these relics, I have come across many another remnant of antiquity, quite as interesting, but of less tangible nature.

Inside a Saxon peasant's house everything is of exemplary neatness, and speaks of welfare. The boards are clean scoured, the window panes shine like crystal. There is no point on which a Saxon

Saxon Peasant at home.

Hausfrau (housewife) is so sensitive as that of order and neatness, and she is visibly put out if surprised by a visit on washing or baking day, when things are not looking quite so trim as usual.

If we happen to come on a week-day, we generally find the best room or *Prunkzimmer* locked up, with darkened shutters, and only on our request to be shown the embroidered pillow-covers and the best jugs reserved for grand occasions, will the hostess half ungraciously proceed to unlock the door and throw open the shutter.

This *Prunkzimmer* takes the place of the state parlour in our Scotch farmhouses; but those latter, with their funereal horse-hair furniture and cheerless polished table, would contrast unfavourably beside these quaintly old-fashioned German apartments. Here the furniture, consisting of benches, bunkers, bedsteads, chest of drawers, and chairs, are painted in lively colours, often festoons of roses and tulips on a ground of dark blue or green: the patterns, frequently bold and striking, if of a somewhat barbaric style of art, betray the Oriental influence of Roumanian country artists, of whom they are doubtless borrowed. A similarly painted wooden framework runs round the top of the room, above the doors and windows, with pegs, from which are suspended the jugs I am in search of, and a bar behind which rows of plates are secured.

On the large unoccupied bedsteads are piled up, sometimes as high as the ceiling, stores of huge downy pillows, their covers richly embroidered in

quaint patterns executed in black, scarlet, or blue
and yellow worsted. They are mostly worked in
the usual tapestry cross-stitch, and often represent flowers, birds, or animals in the old German
style—the name of the embroideress and the date

Saxon Embroidery.

of the work being usually introduced. Many of
the pieces I saw were very old, and dates of the
seventeenth and eighteenth centuries are constant-
ly turning up; but alongside are others of recent

date, for the custom of thus employing the long winter evenings is still kept up among the village girls.

I asked some of them whence they took their patterns? whether they had any sampler books or printed designs to copy from? Nothing of the sort, I was told; they just copy from one another and from old pieces of work. Thus it comes about that many of them to-day go on reproducing some old bird or flower, first introduced by an ancestress of the worker many hundred years ago.

This system of copying is clearly to be traced in the different villages. As each village forms a separate body or community, and intercourse and intermarriage hardly ever take place, these patterns become localised, and one design is apt to run in one particular place to the exclusion of others. Thus I remarked one village where flourishes a peculiar breed of square-built peacocks, alternated with preposterous stags in red and blue worsted, but these fabulous animals are rarely wont to stray beyond the confines of their own parish; while in another community there is a strongly marked epidemic of embroidered double-eagles, perhaps explainable by the fact that part of the population is of Austrian extraction.

The Saxon *Hausfrau* will generally receive us in a surly mistrustful manner, and the Saxon peas-

ant will not dream of rising from his seat when he
sees a lady enter the room. If we happen to be
tired we had better sit down unbidden, for neither
he nor she is likely to offer us a chair.

Our question as to whether they have any jugs
or plates is usually met with a sort of ungracious
affirmative. "Will they sell them?" "Not on
any account whatsoever! these jugs belonged to
some dearly beloved great-grandfather or grand-
mother, and must be preserved in their memory.
Not for unheard-of sums of gold could they bear to
separate themselves from such a relic," &c., &c.

These assertions must, however, be taken for
what they are worth, and whoever has tried the
experiment will have found by experience that it
is merely a question of money, and that sometimes
an extra bid of ten or twenty kreutzers (twopence
or fourpence) will turn the scale, and induce these
pious grandchildren to consign to oblivion the
memory of the beloved ancestor.

These jugs, which are destined to hold wine
(one for each guest) on the occasion of their baptismal, wedding, or funeral banquets, are from nine
to eleven inches high, and have a metal lid attached to the handle. Every variety of colouring
and pattern is to be found among them : sometimes
it is an uncouth design of dancing or drunken peasants, sometimes a pair of stags, or a dog in pursuit

Saxon Embroidery and Pottery.

[To face p. 92.

(This and the illustration on p. 90 are from the collection of Saxon Antiquities in possession of Herr Emil Sigerus at Hermanstadt.)

of a hare, or else a basket filled with fruit, or raised medallions with sprigs of flowers in the centre.

My inquiries were usually met by the suspicious counter-questions, "Why do you want to buy our jugs? What are you going to do with them?" and the answer I gave, that I was fond of such old things, and that they would be hung up in my dining-room, was often received with evident disbelief.

These people are not easily induced to talk about themselves, and have little sense of humour or power of repartee. They have an instinctive distrust of whoever tries to draw them out, scenting in each superfluous question a member of a species they abhor—namely, "a chiel among them taking notes;" or as the Saxon puts it, "one of those incomprehensible town folk, ever fretting and ferreting after our ways and customs, and who have no sensible reason for doing so either."

Two analogous incidents which I met with, soon after my arrival in Transylvania, seemed to give me the respective clues to Saxon and Roumanian character. The first was in a Saxon peasant's house, where I had just purchased two jugs and a plate, for which, being still a stranger in those parts, I had paid considerably more than they were worth, when on leaving the house the hostess put a small bunch of flowers into my hand. The nosegay was somewhat tumbled and faded, for this was

Sunday afternoon, and probably the woman or her daughter had worn these flowers at church earlier in the day. In my ignorance of Saxon character, I took this offering in the light of a courteous attention, and accepted the bouquet with a word of thanks.

My error did not last long, for as I stepped into the courtyard the wooden Noah's-ark faced woman hurried after me, and roughly snatching the nosegay out of my hand, she harshly exclaimed—

"I do not give my flowers for nothing! unless you pay me two kreutzers (a halfpenny), I shall keep them for myself!"

Very much amused, I paid the required sum, feeling that in spite of the crushed condition of the flowers, I had got more than a halfpenny's worth out of my hostess after all.

Two or three days later, when out riding, we lost our way in the mazes of the Yungwald, the large oak-forest which stretches for miles over the country to the south of Hermanstadt. It was near sunset when we found ourselves in a totally strange neighbourhood, not knowing which turn to take in order to regain the road back to town. Just then a Roumanian peasant woman came in sight. She had on her back a bundle of firewood, which she had probably stolen in the forest, and in her hand she carried a large bunch of purple iris flowers, fresh and dripping from some neighbouring marsh.

I suppose that I must have looked longingly at
the beautiful purple bunch, for while my husband
was asking the way as well as he could by means
of a little broken Italian, she came round to the
side of my horse, and with a pretty gesture held
up the flowers for my acceptance. With the Saxon
lesson fresh in my mind, I hesitated to take them,
for I had left my purse at home; so I explained to
her by pantomime that I had no money about me.
She had not been thinking of money, it seems, and
energetically disclaimed the offer of payment, con-
tinuing her way after a courteous " *buna sara* "
(good evening).

Since then, in my walks and rides about Hermanstadt I have often been presented with similar
offerings from perfectly unknown Roumanian peasants, who would sometimes stop their galloping
horses and get out of the cart merely for the
purpose of giving me a few flowers; but never,
never has it been my good luck to receive the
smallest sign of spontaneous courtesy from any
Saxon, and I grieve to say that frequently my experience has been all the other way.

One day, for instance, when walking in a hay-
field through which ran a rapid mill-stream, I
suddenly missed my dog, a lively rat-terrier, who
had been running backwards and forwards in search
of field-mice. " Brick, Brick, Brick," I called in

vain over and over again, but Brick was nowhere
to be seen. Only a stifled squealing, apparently
proceeding from the mill-stream some way off, met
my ear; but I did not immediately think of connecting this sound with my truant terrier. Some
Saxon peasants were at work near the water stow-
ing up hay on to a cart. " Have you not seen my
dog ? " I called out to them.

One of the men now slowly removed his pipe
from his mouth. " Your dog ? " he asked, stolidly.
" Oh yes; he's just drowning yonder in the stream."
And he lazily pointed over his shoulder with a
pitchfork.

I rushed to the bank, and there sure enough was
my poor half-drowned Brick struggling to keep
himself above water, but almost exhausted already.
He had fallen in over the treacherous edge, which
was masked by overhanging bushes, and the banks
being too steep to effect a landing, he must inevitably have perished had I not come up in time.
With considerable difficulty, and at the risk of falling in myself, I managed to drag him out, the
worthy Saxons meanwhile looking on with indolent
enjoyment, never dreaming of offering assistance.

The hard and grasping characters of the Saxons
appear in every detail of their daily life; they taint
their family relations, and would almost seem to
put a marketable price on the most sacred affec-

tions. Thus a Saxon mother in her cradle-song informs the sleeping infant that she values it as high as a hundred florins; while the grief over a beloved corpse often takes the form of counting up the exact pecuniary loss to the family sustained from the decease.

Their family life does not appear to be happy, and divorces are lamentably numerous. It seems, in fact, as if divorce had grown to be an established habit among these people ; and despite all efforts of the clergy to discourage this abuse, and the difficulties purposely put in the way of divorcing parties, there is little prospect of improvement as yet. No improvement can possibly take place till Saxon parents give up forcing their children to wed against their will, merely for mercenary reasons, and till girls are allowed to attain a reasonable age before binding themselves down to a contract of such importance. When want of sympathy towards the proposed husband is urged on the part of the girl, such objections are usually settled by the practical advice of the long-sighted parents. " Try him for a time, and maybe you will get to like him ; and if not— well, the misfortune is none so great, and you can always seek for a divorce." Brides of fifteen are quite on the order of the day, and few are suffered to reach so mature an age as seventeen or eighteen ; the consequence of these arrangements being that fully a third of the couples go asunder, each choosing another mate, with whom they usually fare better than with their first venture.

Often in the course of my visits to Saxon peasant houses have I come across one of these unfortunate young females returned to her parents' house, sometimes after a few weeks only of matrimony, there to await the divorce which is to set her free to choose again.

The reasons which induce these people to sue for a separation are frequently so exceedingly futile and ridiculous as hardly to deserve that name. Often it is the food which is made a cause of complaint—either the husband declaring that his wife will take no trouble to please him with her cookery, or else the wife complaining of his being capricious and hard to please. An underdone potato may prove so very indigestible as to sever the conjugal bond, or an ill-baked loaf of bread assume such dimensions as to constitute a barrier for life.

Village pastors whose parishes lie in the wine-bearing districts, affirm that the season immediately following upon the vintage, when the cellars are full of new wine, is the most quarrelsome time in the year, and the one which engenders most separations. But even without the aid of stimulants, and when no thought of divorce is in their minds, quarrelsome *ménages* are numerous, and the old story of the Tartar carrying off the shrewish wife of a thoroughly resigned husband may well have had its origin here. This legend, told all over Hungary, relates how a peasant, as he calmly watched the retreating figure of the Tartar bearing off the wife of his bosom, was heard to murmur, "Poor Tartar! thou hast made a bad bargain."

In Transylvania this same story is told of a Saxon peasant, but with a sequel; for this version relates how the bereaved widower settled himself down to a hearty supper that same evening, ever and anon murmuring, as his eye rested on the empty chair opposite his own, the words, "Poor Tartar!" for he was a kind-hearted man, and felt compassion even for the sufferings of a barbarian. But of a sudden the door flies open, and the wretched man once more beholds his lost wife standing before him. Her temper had proved too much even for a Tartar, who had wisely flown, leaving his captive behind.

The words "Poor Tartar!" now gave place to another form of ejaculation; and whenever he deemed himself out of earshot, the Saxon muttered bitterly between his teeth, "Rascally Tartar! Rascally Tartar!"

But for this unfortunate *dénouement*, who knows

whether Saxon husbands of to-day might not frequently be moved to regret the good old times
when an obliging Tartar might be expected thus to
relieve them of such superfluous blessings.

The bond between parent and child seems to be
hardly more commendable. Perhaps my experience has been exceptionally infelicitous, but certainly never in any country has it been my ill-
fortune to listen to such shocking and disrespectful
language from children to their parents, as what I
have occasionally overheard in Saxon cottages.

The Saxon peasant being a declared enemy of
large families, presents a striking contrast to his
Roumanian neighbour, with whom six or eight
bairns are a very common allowance, and who
regards each new addition to the family as another
gift of God. The oft-repeated insinuation that
the Transylvanian Saxons seek to limit their progeny by unnatural means, does not seem to be
entirely without foundation. It is said that to
have two children only is considered the correct
thing in a Saxon household, and that the Saxon
mother who, when cross-questioned as to her offspring, has to acknowledge three bairns, turns away
her head shamefacedly, as though she were confess-
ing a crime.

It is because the Saxon does not care to see his
fields cut up into small sections that he desires his

family to be small; and the consequence of this short-sighted egotism is, that the population of many villages shows a yearly decrease, and that houses often stand empty because there is no one to live there.[1] Thus one village near Hermanstadt can show twenty-seven, another twelve such deserted dwellings. A man whose whole family consisted of two daughters, both married to peasants with houses of their own, was asked what would become of his fine well-built home after his decease. " It will just stand empty," was the stolid reply. In some villages these empty Saxon houses have been taken possession of by Roumanians, who look strangely incongruous within these massive stone walls, reminding one somehow of sparrows which have taken up their residence in a deserted rookery.

Saxon political economists, alive to the danger of their race becoming extinct, think of trying to get new batches of German colonists to settle here, in order to freshen up and increase the number of the race; but there is little chance of such projects being successful. The inducements which formerly tempted strangers no longer exist; and there are probably few Germans who would think it worth

---

[1] This abuse, however, is entirely confined to the villages, the towns showing a far more favourable rate of increase among the Saxon population.

their while to settle in a country where every inch
of land has already been appropriated, and where
the Government seeks to rob each one of his
nationality.

The besetting fault of this whole Saxon nation
seems to be an immoderate spirit of egotism, so
short-sighted as frequently to defeat its own end,
leading each man to consider only his individual
welfare, to the exclusion of every other feeling.
It is strange and paradoxical that these honest,
moral, thrifty, industrious, and educated Saxons
should live thus in their well-built roomy houses
in a constant state of inward dissension and strife ;
while their neighbours, the poor, ignorant, thieving
Roumanians, crowded together in their wretched
hovels, are united by the bonds of a most touching
family affection.[1]

---

[1] The assertion that the Transylvanian Saxons—taken as a body
—show a yearly decrease, is however incorrect, as has been con-
clusively proved by Dr Oskar von Meltzl, in his recent interesting
work, ' Statistik der Sächsischen Landbevölkerung in Siebenbürgen.'
By the author's own acknowledgment, however, the increase within
the last thirty-two years has been but insignificant ; while of 227
Saxon communities established in the country, 92 have diminished
in number between the years 1851-1883 to the extent of nearly 11
per cent.

Fortified Saxon Church.

[To face p. 102.

CHAPTER IX.

SAXON CHURCHES AND SIEGES.

THE words "church" and "fortress" used to be synonymous in Transylvania, so the places of worship might accurately have been described as churches militant. Each Saxon village church was surrounded by a row, sometimes even a double or triple row, of fortified walls, which are mostly still extant. The remains of moat and drawbridge are also yet frequently to be seen. When threatened by an enemy, the people used to retire into these fortresses, often built on some rising piece of ground, taking with them their valuables as well as provisions for the contingency of a lengthy siege. From these heights the Saxons used to roll down heavy stones on to their assailants, sometimes with terrible effect; but when they had in this way exhausted their missiles, the predicament was often a very precarious one. Some of these stones still survive, and may occasionally be seen

—as within the fortress walls of the old ruined
church which I have already mentioned as standing on a steep incline above the picturesque village
of Michelsberg.

The church itself, having been replaced by a
more conveniently situated one down in the village,
is now deserted, and is used only as a storehouse by
the villagers.   The fortified walls are crumbling
away, and the passage round the church is choked
up by weeds and briers, amongst which lie strewn
about many old moss-grown stones, circular in shape
and resembling giant cannon-balls.   These were the
missiles which lay there in readiness to be rolled
down on to an approaching enemy; and there was
a law compelling each bridegroom, before leading
his bride to the altar, to roll uphill to the church-
door one of these formidable globes.   This was so
ordained in order to exclude from matrimony all
sick or weakly subjects; and as the incline was a
steep one, and each stone weighed about two
hundredweight, it was a considerable test of
strength.

Would that these old stones, lying here neglected
among the nettles, had the gift of speech !   What
traits of love and of bloodshed might we not learn
from them !   Only to look at them there strewn
around, it is not difficult to guess at the outlines of
some of the stories they are dumbly telling us.

Many are chipped and worn away, and have evidently been used more than once in their double capacity, alternately rolled up the hill by smiling Cupid, to be hurled down again by furious Nemesis.

Here near a clump of burdock-leaves is a shabby-looking globe of yellow sandstone, whose puny size plainly speaks of a *mariage de convenance*— a mere union of hands without hearts: perhaps some old widower, with trembling hands and shaky knees, in quest of a wife to look after his house, and to whom the whole matter was very uphill work indeed!

Close alongside, half hidden beneath the graceful tangles of a wild-rose bush, is a formidable boulder of gigantic, nay, heroic size, which forcibly suggests that it must have been a mighty love indeed which brought it up here—so mighty, no doubt, that to the two strong young arms which rolled it up the hill it must have seemed light as a feather's weight.

And how many of these, might one ask, have been rolled up here in vain, in so far as the love was concerned? When the fire of love had grown cold and its sweetness all turned to vinegar, how many, many a former lover must heartily have wished that he had never moved his stone from the bottom of the hill!

Such thoughts involuntarily crowd on the mind

when sitting, as I have done many a time, within this lonely ruin on fine summer evenings, the idyllic peacefulness of the scene the more strongly felt by contrast with the bloody memories linked around it. It is so strange to realise how completely everything has passed away that once used to be: that the hands which pushed these heavy globes, as well as the Moslem crania for which they were intended, have turned alike to dust; that hushed for ever are the voices once awaking fierce echoes within these very walls; and that of all those contrasting passions, of all that tender love and that burning hatred, nothing has survived but a few old stones lying forgotten near a deserted church!

The history of the sieges endured in Transylvania on the part of Turk or Tartar would in itself furnish matter for many volumes. Numberless anecdotes are yet current characterising the endurance and courage of the besieged, and the original means often resorted to in order to baffle or mislead the enemy.

Once it was the ready wit of a Szekel woman which saved her people besieged by the Tartars within the Almescher cavern. As the whole land had been devastated from end to end, a severe famine was the consequence, and both besiegers and besieged were sorely in want of victuals. The Szekels had taken some provisions with them into the cave, but these were soon exhausted; and the Tartars, though starving themselves, were consoled by thinking that hunger would soon compel their enemy to give in. One day, when, as usual, the barbarians had assembled shouting and howling in front of the cavern, whose entrance was defended by a high wall, a Hungarian woman held up before their eyes a large cake at the end of a long pole, and cried out tauntingly, " See here, ye dogs of Tartars! Thus are we feasting in plenty and comfort, while you are reduced to eat grass and roots of trees." This much vaunted cake was but kneaded together of water and ashes, with a few last remaining spoonfuls of flour; but the Tartars, taken in by the feint, abandoned the field.

Another time, it was nothing more than a swarm of bees which turned the scale in favour of the Saxons, hard pressed by the enemy outside. Already they had begun to scale the walls of the fortified church, and death and destruction seemed imminent, when the youthful daughter of the churchwarden was struck by a bright idea. Behind the church was a little garden full of sweet-scented flowers, and containing a dozen bee-hives, which it was Lieschen's (such was her name) pride to watch over. Seizing a hive in each hand, she sprang up on the fortress wall, and with all her strength hurled them down amongst the approaching besiegers. Again and again she repeated this manœuvre till the hives were exhausted, and the bewildered enemies, blinded by the dense swarm of infuriated bees, deafened by the angry buzzing in their ears, and maddened by hundredfold stings, beat an ignominious and hasty retreat.

This occurred in the village of Holzmengen towards the end of the seventeenth century, and of this same village it is related that, when peace was finally restored to the land, the population was so reduced that most houses stood empty. Of four hundred landholders there used to be, but fifteen now remained; and many years passed by without any wedding being celebrated in the place. When, however, at last this rare event came to pass, the bridegroom received the name of the " young man," which stuck to him until his end. The bride was no other than Lieschen, the bee-maiden, and Thomas was the name of her husband; and to this day, whoever is in possession of that particular house goes by the name of *" den jung mon Thomas,"* even though he happen to have been christened Hans or Peter, and be, moreover, as old as Methuselah. If you ask the name of such another house in the same village, you are told that it belongs to *Michel am Eck* (Michael at the corner). It is not a corner house, neither does its proprietor answer to the name of Michel; but where it stands was once the corner of a street, and Michel the name of one of the fifteen land-holders who divided the property after the war —hence the appellation.

There is a story told of an active Saxon house-wife, who, after she had been shut up for three days within the fortress awaiting the Tartars re-ported to be near, began to weary of her enforced idleness, and throwing open the gate of the citadel, impatiently called out, "Now, then, you dogs of Tartars, are you never coming?"

When the Tartars had succeeded in capturing prisoners, they used to fatten them up for eating. A woman from the village of Almesch, being sickly, refused to fatten, and, set at liberty, came home to relate the doleful tale. The little Hungarians and Saxons were regarded as toys for the young Tar-tars, who, setting them up in rows, used to practise upon them the merry pastime of cutting off heads.

Living in Transylvania, we are sometimes inclined to wonder whether to be besieged by Turks and Tartars be really a thing of the past, and not rather an actual danger for which we must be prepared any day, so strangely are many little observances relat-ing to those times still kept up. Thus in the belfry tower at Kaisd there hangs a little bell bearing a

Gothic inscription and the date 1506.   It is rung every evening at the usual curfew-hour, and until within a very few years ago, the watchman was under the obligation of calling forth into the night with stentorian voice, "Not this way, you villains! not this way!   I see you well!"

Also the habit of keeping provisions stored up within the fortified church-walls, to this day extant in most Saxon villages, is clearly a remnant of the time when sieges had to be looked for.   Even now the people seem to consider their goods to be in greater security here than in their own barns and lofts. The outer fortified wall round the church is often divided off into deep recesses or alcoves, in each of which stands a large wooden chest securely locked, and filled with grain or flour, while the little surrounding turrets or chapels are used as storehouses for home-cured bacon.   "We have seven chapels all full of bacon," I was once proudly informed by a village churchwarden; but, with the innate mistrust of his race, he would not indulge my further curiosity on the subject by suffering me to inspect the interior of these greasy sanctuaries, evidently suspecting me of sinister intentions on his bacon stores.

This storing up of provisions is a perfect mania among the Saxons, and each village has its own special hobby or favourite article, vast quantities of which it hoards up in a preposterous, senseless fashion, reminding one of a dog who buries more bones than he can ever hope to eat in the course of his life. Thus, one village prides itself on having the greatest quantity of bacon, much of which is already thirty or forty years old, and consequently totally unfit for use ; while in another community the oldest grain is the great *specialité*. Each article, case, or barrel is marked with the brand of the owner, and the whole placed under the charge of the churchwarden.

Some parishes can still boast of many curiously wrought pieces of church plate remaining over from Catholic days—enamelled chalices, bejewelled crucifixes, remonstrances, and ciboriums, richly inlaid and embossed. The village of Heltau is in possession of many such valuable ornaments, which, during the Turkish wars, used to be buried in the earth, sometimes for a period of many years, the exact spot where the treasure was hidden being known only to the oldest churchwarden, who was careful to pass on the secret to the next in rank when he felt himself to be drawing near the end of his life. Thus, in the year 1794, the church at Heltau, struck by lightning, was seriously dam-aged, and urgently demanded extensive repairs. How to defray these expenses was the question which sorely perplexed the village pastor and the church elders, when the old warden came forward and offered to reveal to the pastor and the second warden the secret of a hidden treasure of whose existence none but he was aware. The man himself had never set eyes on the treasure, but had received from his predecessor precise directions how to find it in case of necessity. Accordingly, under his guidance the pastor, accompanied by the younger warden, repaired to the church, where, entering the right-hand aisle, the old man pointed to three high-backed wooden seats fixed against the wall, saying, "The centre one of these chairs has a movable panel, behind which a door is said to be concealed." After some effort— for the panel was jammed from long disuse — it yielded, moving upwards, and disclosing a small iron door with a keyhole, into which fitted an old-fashioned rusty key produced by the warden. When this door was at last got open, the three men stepped into a small vault paved with bricks. "One of these bricks is marked by a cross, and under it we have to dig for the treasure," were the further instructions given by the old man. A very few minutes proved the truth of his words, bringing to light a small wooden chest containing a chalice, a silver remonstrance, and various other valuables, which may still be seen at the Heltau parsonage; likewise a bag of gold and silver coins, dating from the time of the Batorys, which leads to the supposition that the treasure had been lying here concealed ever since the beginning of the seventeenth century.

Great was the pastor's surprise and delight at this unexpected windfall; but he only took from the bag sufficient money for the necessary repairs, replacing the rest of the treasure where it had been found. None of the other parishioners were informed whence had come the money, so the secret remained a secret.

Only many years later, in the present century, when the son-in-law of the former clergyman had become pastor in his turn, the story of the treasure was imparted to him by the successor of former wardens. The necessity for concealment had now gone by, and peace and prosperity reigned in the country; so the church ornaments were once more disinterred, and finally restored to the light of day, while the antiquated gold and silver pieces, exchanged into current coinage, were applied to useful purposes. Thus it was that the secret oozed out, and came to be generally known.

Saxon village churches of the present day are generally bare and unornamented inside, for all decorations had been dismantled at the time of the Reformation; stone niches have been emptied

of the statues they contained, and rich pieces of
carving stowed away in lumber-rooms. Only the
old oriental carpets, brought hither from Turkish
campaigns, which frequently adorn the front of the
pews or the organ-gallery, have been suffered to
remain, and hang there still, delicately harmonious in colouring, but riddled through with holes
like a sieve, and fed upon by the descendants
of a hundred generations of moths, which flutter
in a dense cloud round the visitor who inadver-
tently raises a corner of the drapery to investigate
its fleecy quality.

Curious old tombstones and bas-reliefs may often
be seen carelessly huddled together in the church
entrance or outside the walls, treated with no sort
of appreciation of their historical value or care for
their ultimate preservation. Also the numerous
frescoes which used to cover many church walls
have been obliterated by the barbarous touch of a
whitewashing hand. It would almost seem as if
this Saxon people had originally possessed some
degree of artistic feeling, which has been, however,
effectually extinguished by the Reformation; for
it is difficult otherwise to explain how a nation
capable of raising monuments of real artistic value
in the troubled times of the barbarous middle
ages, should be thus heedless of their conservation
in the present enlightened and peaceful century.

Of this lamentable indifference to the conservation of their historical and artistic treasures, the ruined Abbey of Kerz, situated in the valley of the

Ruined Abbey of Kerz.

Aluta, offers a melancholy instance.   This wealthy Cistercian monastery was founded by King Bela III. towards the end of the twelfth century ; but being abolished by King Mathias three centuries later, on account of irregularities into which the monks had fallen, it passed, with its lands, into possession of the Hermanstadt church.

The choir of the ancient abbey church, built in the time of Louis the Great in the transition style,

is still used as a place of worship by the small
Lutheran congregation of Kerz, but the nave has
been suffered to fall into decay: many of the
richly carved stones of which it was formed have
been carried off by the villagers, who have utilised
them for building their houses, or degraded them
to yet baser purposes. We ourselves crossed the
little stream, which runs close by the parson's
house, on stepping-stones evidently taken from
the ancient building. Likewise a lime-tree of
gigantic dimensions in front of the western portal,
and supposed to have been planted when the foundation - stone of the church was laid, is now in
imminent danger of splitting in twain for want
of the trifling attention of an iron waist-band to
keep its poor old body together. Such the present
lamentable condition of one of the most interesting
relics in the country, which has been named the
Melrose of Transylvania.

CHAPTER X.

THE SAXON VILLAGE PASTOR.

THE contrast between the domestic lives of Roumanian and Saxon peasants is all the more surprising, as their respective clergies set totally different examples; for while many Roumanian priests are drunken, dissolute men, open to every sort of bribery, the Saxon pastor is almost invariably a model of steadiness and morality, and leads a quiet, industrious, and contented life.

On the other hand, however, it may be remarked that if the Saxon pastor be steady and well behaved, he has very good and solid reasons for so being. Certainly he is most comfortably indemnified for the virtues he is expected to practise.

When a pastor dies, the villagers themselves elect his successor by votes. Usually it is a man whom they know already by sight or reputation, or from having heard him preach on stray occasions in their church. Every Saxon pastor, in order to

be qualified for the position, must have practised
for several years as professor at a public gymnasium
—a very wise regulation, as it ensures the places
being filled by men of education.

The part which a village pastor is called upon to
 play requires both
head and heart,
for the relation
between shepherd
and flock is here
very different from
the conventional
footing on which
clergy and laity
stand with regard
to each other in
town life. Where-
as in the city no
congregation cares
to see its spiritual
head outside the
church walls, and
would resent as
unpardonable in-

Saxon Pastor in full dress.

trusion any attempt of his to penetrate the privacy
of the domestic circle, the villager not only expects
but insists on his pastor taking intimate part in
his family life, and being ready to assist him

with advice and admonition in every possible
contingency.

The peasants are therefore very circumspect
about the choice of a pastor, well aware that the
weal or woe of a community may depend upon
the selection. They have often seen how some
neighbouring village has awakened to new life and
prosperity since the advent of a worthy clergyman ;
while such another parish, from a rash selection,
has saddled itself with a man it would fain cart
away as so much useless straw, were it only possible
to get rid of him. For although the power of
choice lies entirely with the peasants, they cannot
likewise undo their work at will, and only the
bishop has power to depose a pastor, when he has
investigated the complaints brought against him
and found them to be justified.

Not only the pastor *in spe* but also his wife
is carefully scrutinised, and her qualifications for
the patriarchal position she has to occupy critically
examined into; for if the clergyman is termed by
his flock " the honourable father," so is she designated as the " virtuous mother." The candidate
who happens to have a thrifty and benevolent
consort, finds his chances of election considerably
enhanced; while such another, married to a vain
and frivolous woman, will most likely be found
awanting when weighed in the balance.

The funeral of a village pastor has been touch-ingly described by a native author,[1] whose words I take the liberty of quoting :—

" The old father had gone to his long rest : more than once during the last few years he had felt that the time had come for him to lay down the shep-herd's crook, for the world had become too stirring, and he no longer had the strength and activity of spirit to do all that was expected of him.   There were serious repairs to be undertaken about the church, and the question of building a new school-house was becoming urgent.   Likewise many of the new church regulations were harassing and dis-tasteful exceedingly : most especially was he trou-bled by inward quakings at the idea, that at the bishop's next official visit he would be expected to submit to him the MSS. of all the sermons he had preached within the year, and which, neatly tied up together with black worsted, were lying on the lowest shelf of the bookcase.

" All these thoughts had reconciled him to the prospect of death, and when sitting before his door on fine summer evenings he would sometimes re-mark to the neighbours who had lingered near for a passing chat,—' It cannot last over long with me now : one or two pair of soles at most I shall wear out, and I should be glad to remain in the village,

[1] Dr Fronius.

and to sleep there under the big lime-tree, in the
midst of those with whom my life has been spent.
Therefore kindly bear with me a little longer, good
people, for the few remaining days the Lord is
pleased to spare me.' And these words never failed
to conciliate even the more turbulent spirits, who
were apt to think that the Herr Vater was over
long in going, and that the parish stood in need
of a younger head.

" Now at last the coffin has been lowered into
the earth, and the fresh mound covered with dewy
garlands of flowers. All the villagers have turned
out to render the last honours to the father they
have lost. The eldest son of the defunct, standing
near the grave, addresses the congregation. In a
few simple words he thanks them for the good they
have done to his father and to his whole family,
and, in name of the dead man, he begs their forgiveness for whatever wrongs the pastor may un-
wittingly have done ; and when he then lays down
the keys of both church and parsonage into the
hand of the churchwarden, scarcely an eye will
remain dry among the spectators. For forty years
is a long time in which a good man, even though
he often errs and be at fault, can yet have done
much, very much, good indeed, and resentment is
a plant which strikes no root in the upturned clods
of a new-made grave."

But the orphaned congregation must have a new
pastor,—the flock cannot be suffered to remain long
without a shepherd ; and this is the topic which is
being discussed with much warmth at an assemblage
of village elders.   On the white-decked table are
standing dishes of bread and cheese, flanked by
large tankards of wine.   The first glass has just
been emptied to the memory of the dead pastor,
and now the second glass will be drunk to the
health of his yet unknown successor.

These meetings, preceding the election of a new
shepherd, are often long and stormy, for when the
wine has taken effect and loosened the tongues, the
different candidates who might be taken into consideration are passed in review, and extolled with
much heat, or abused with broad sarcasm.   One
man is rejected on account of an impediment in his
speech, and another because he is known to be
unmarried : a third one, who might do well enough
for any other parish, cannot be chosen here because
his old parents are natives of the village—for it is
a true, though a hard, word which says, that no
one can be a prophet in his own country.   One man
who ventures to suggest the vicar of a neighbouring village is informed that no blacker traitor
exists on the face of the earth ; and another, who
describes his pet candidate as an ideal clergyman,
with the figure of a Hercules and the voice of a

Stentor, is ironically asked whether he wishes to choose a pastor by weight and measure? If only his head and heart be in the right place, the clergyman's legs are welcome to be an inch or two shorter.

After a longer or shorter interval, a decision is finally arrived at. From a list of six candidates, one has been elected by the secret votes of the community, each married landowner having a voice in the matter, and the name of the successful aspirant is publicly made known in church. Meanwhile a group of young men on horseback are waiting at the church door, and hardly has the all-important name been pronounced when they set spurs to their steeds and gallop to bear the news to the successful candidate. A hot race ensues, for the foremost one can hope to get a shining piece of silver—perhaps even gold—in exchange for the good tidings he brings. In a carriage, at a more leisurely pace, follow the elders who have been deputed to hand over the official document containing the nomination.

An early day is fixed for the presentation of the new shepherd to his flock, and at a still earlier date the new Frau Pastorin precedes him thither, where she is soon deep in the mysteries of cake-baking, fowl-killing, &c., &c., in view of the many official banquets which are to accompany the presentation.

In this employment she has ample assistance from the village matrons, as well as contributions of eggs, cream, butter, and bacon. The day before the presentation the pastor has been fetched in a carriage drawn by six white horses. The first step to his installation is the making out and signing of the agreement or treaty between pastor and people, —all the said pastor's duties, obligations, and privileges being therein distinctly specified and enumerated, from the exact quantity and quality of Holy Gospel he is bound to administer yearly to the congregation, down to his share of wild crab-apples for brewing the household vinegar, and the precise amount of acorns his pigs are at liberty to consume.

After this treaty has been duly signed and read aloud, the keys of the church are solemnly given over and accepted with appropriate speeches. The banquet which succeeds this ceremony is called the " key-drinking." Then follows the solemn installation in the church, where the new pastor, for the first time, pronounces aloud the blessing over his congregation, who strain their ears with critical attention to catch the sound and pass sentence thereon. The Saxon peasant thinks much of a full sonorous voice; therefore woe to the man who is cursed with a thin squeaky organ, for he will assuredly fall at least fifty per cent in the estimation of his audience.

Then follows another banquet, at which each of the church officials has his place at table marked by a silver thaler piece (about 3s.) lying at the bottom of his large tankard, and visible through the clear golden wine with which the bumper is filled. Etiquette demands that the drinker should taste of the wine but sparingly at first, merely wetting the lips and affecting not to perceive the silver coin ; but when the health of the new pastor is drunk, each man must empty his tankard at one draught, skilfully catching the thaler between the teeth, as he drains it dry. This coin is then supposed to be treasured up in memory of the event.

This has been but a flying visit to his new parish, and only some weeks later does the new pastor hold his solemn entry into the parish, the preparations for the flitting naturally occupying some few weeks. The village is bound to convey the new pastor, his family, as well as all their goods and chattels, to the new home, and it is considered a distinction when many carts are required for the purpose, even though the distance be great and the roads bad, for the people would have no opinion at all of a pastor who arrived in light marching order, but seem rather to value him in proportion to the trouble he gives them. As many as eighteen to twenty carts are sometimes pressed into service for this patriarchal procession.

The six white horses which are to be harnessed to the carriage for the clergyman and his wife have been carefully fattened up during the last few weeks, their manes plaited with bright ribbons, and the carriage itself decorated with flower garlands. At the parish boundary all the young men of the village have come out on horseback to meet them, and with flying banners they ride alongside of the carriage. In this way the village is reached, where sometimes a straw rope is stretched across the road to bar his entrance. This is removed on the pastor paying a ransom, and, entering the village, the driver is expected to conduct his horses at full gallop thrice round the fortified walls of the church before entering the parsonage courtyard.

The village pastor, who lives among his people, must adopt their habits and their hours. It would not do for him to lie abed till seven or eight o'clock, like a town gentleman : five o'clock, and even sooner, must find him dressed and ready to attend to the hundred and one requirements of his parishioners, who, even at that early hour, come pouring in upon him from all sides.

Perhaps it is a petition for some particularly fine sort of turnip-seed, which only the Herr Vater has got; or else he is requested to look into his wise book to see if he can find a remedy for the stubborn cough of a favourite horse, or the distressing state

of the calf's digestion. Another will bring him a
dish of golden honeycomb, with some question regarding the smoking of the hives; while a fourth
has come to request the pastor to transform his
new-born son from a Pagan into a Christian infant.

Various deputations of villagers, inviting the
pastor to two different funerals and to six weddings, have successively been disposed of: then
will come a peasant with some Hungarian legal
document which he would like to have deciphered.
Has he won the lawsuit which has been pending
these two years and more? or has he lost it, and
will he be obliged to pay the damages as well?
This is a riddle which only the Herr Vater can
read him aright, by consulting the big Hungarian
dictionary on the shelf.

The next visitor is perchance an old white-
bearded man, bent double with the weight of years,
and carrying a well-worn Bible under his arm. He
wants to know his age, which used to be entered
somewhere here in the book; but he cannot find
the place, or else the bookbinder, in mending the
volume last year, has pasted paper over it. Perhaps the Herr Vater can make it out for him; and
further to facilitate the search, he mentions that
there was corn in the upper fields, and maize in the
low meadows, the year he was born, and that since
then the corn has been sown twenty-four times on

the same spot, and will be sown there again next
year if God pleases to spare him.   The pastor, who
must of course be well versed in this sort of rural
arithmetic, has no difficulty in pronouncing the
man to be exactly seventy-three years and three
months old, and sends him away well pleased to
discover that he is a whole year younger than he
had believed himself to be.

Often, too, a couple appear on the scene for the
purpose of being reconciled.   The man has beaten
his wife, and she has come to complain—not of the
beating in the abstract, but of the manner in which
this particular castigation has been administered.
It was really too bad this time, as, sobbing, she
explains to the Herr Vater that he has belaboured
her with a thick leather thong in a truly heathen-
ish fashion, instead of taking the broomstick, as
does every respectable man, to beat his wife.

The virtuous Frau Mutter has likewise her full
share of the day's work.   An old hen to be made
into broth for a sick grandchild, a piece of cloth to
be cut out in the shape of a jacket, or a handkerchief to be hemmed on the big sewing-machine,
all pass successively into her busy hands; and if
she goes for a day's shopping to the nearest market
town, she is positively besieged by commissions of
all sorts.   Six china plates of some particular pattern, a coffee cup to replace the one thrown down

by the cat last week, a pound of loaf-sugar, the whitest, finest, sweetest, and cheapest that can be got, or a packet of composition candles. Even weightier matters are sometimes intrusted to her judgment, and she may have to accept the awful responsibility of selecting a new mirror or a petroleum lamp.

Letter-writing is also another important branch of the duties of both pastor and wife. It may be an epistle to some daughter who is in service, or to a soldier son away with his regiment, a threatening letter to an unconscientious debtor, or a business transaction with the farmer of another village. In fact, all the raw material of epistolary affection, remonstrance, counsel, or threat, is brought wholesale to the parsonage, there to be fashioned into shape, and set forth clearly in black upon white.

Altogether the day of a Saxon pastor is a busy and well-filled one, for his doors, from sunrise to sunset, must be open to his parishioners, so that after having "risen with the lark," he is well content further to carry out the proverb by " going to bed with the lamb."

A great deal of patience and natural tact is requisite to enable a clergyman to deal intelligently with his folk. His time must always be at their disposal, and he must never appear to be hurried or busy when expected to listen to some long-winded story or complaint. Nothing must be too trifling to arouse his interest, and no hour of the day too unreasonable to receive a visit; yet, on the whole, the lot of such a village pastor who rightly understands his duties, seems to me a very peaceful and enviable one. He is most comfortably situated as regards material welfare, and stands sufficiently aside from the bustling outer world to be spared the annoyances and irritations of more ambitious careers. The fates of his parishioners, so closely interwoven with his own, are a constant source of interest, and the almost unlimited power he enjoys within the confines of his parish makes him feel himself to be indeed the monarch of this little kingdom.

One parsonage in particular is engraved on my mind as a perfect frame for such Arcadian happiness. An old-fashioned roomy house, with high-pitched roof, it stands within the ring of fortified walls which encircle the church as well. A few wide-spreading lime-trees are picturesquely dotted about the turf between the two buildings; and some old moss-grown stones half sunk in the velvet grass where the violets cluster so thick in spring, betray this to be the site of a long-disused burying-place. Up a few steps there is a raised platform with seats arranged against the wall, from which, as from an opera-box, one may overlook the village

street and mark the comings and goings of the
inhabitants; and a large kitchen-garden, opening
through the wall in another direction, contains
every fruit and vegetable which a country heart
can desire. But the greatest attraction, to my
thinking, was a long arcade of lilac bushes, so
thickly grown that the branches closed together
overhead, only admitting a soft tremulous green
half light, and scented with every variety of the
dear old-fashioned shrub, from the exquisite dwarf
Persian and snowy white, to each possible gradation
of lilac pink and pinky lilac. Along this fragrant
gallery old carved stone benches are placed at intervals; and hither, as the venerable pastor informed me, he always comes on Saturday evenings
in summer to compose his sermon for the morrow.
" It is so much easier to think out here," he said,
" among the birds and flowers and the old graves
all around. When the air is scented with the breath
of violets, and from the open church window comes
the sound of the organ, ah, then I feel myself another man, and God teaches me quite other words
to say to my people than those I find for myself
inside the house ! "

CHAPTER XI.

THE SAXON BROTHERHOODS—NEIGHBOURHOODS AND VILLAGE HANN.

AMONGST the curiosities I picked up in the course of my wanderings about Saxon villages, is a large zinc dish sixteen inches in diameter, curiously engraved and inscribed. On the outside rim there is a running pattern of hares and stags; on the inside a coat of arms, and this inscription—

> "NEU JAHRS GESCHENK VON DER
> EHRLICHEN BRUDERSCHAFT.[1]
> ALT GESEL GEORG BAYR;
> JUNGER TOMAS FRAYTAG.
> 1791."

The dish makes a convenient tray for holding calling-cards, and its origin is an interesting addition to the history of these Saxon people, as it comprises two noteworthy features of their organisation — namely, the Bruderschaften (brotherhoods), and the Nachbarschaften (neighbourhoods).

[1] New-Year's gift from the honourable brotherhood.

The Bruderschaft is an association to which belong all young men of the parish, from the date of
their confirmation up to that of their marriage.
This community is governed by strict laws, in
which the duties of its members respectively, as
citizens, sons, brothers, suitors, and even dancers,
are distinctly traced out. In their outward form
these brotherhoods have some sort of resemblance
to the religious confraternities still existing in
many Catholic countries, and most probably they
originated in the same manner ; but while these
latter have now degenerated into mere outward
forms, the Saxon brotherhoods have retained the
original spirit of such institutions, principally consisting in the reciprocal watch its members kept
over each other's morality. Mr Boner, in his book,
very aptly compares the Saxon Bruderschaften to
the Heidelberg Burschenschafts ; and spite of the
great difference which may at first sight appear,
these institutions are the only ones to which the
Saxon brotherhoods may at all be likened. In the
towns these confraternities have now completely
disappeared, but in villages they are still in full
force, and have but little or nothing of their
original character.[1]

[1] The late King of Bavaria, Ludwig II., made an attempt at re-
viving these brotherhoods, such as they existed in Germany in the
middle ages. He himself was the head of the confraternity, and
designed the costumes to be worn by its members, who, with their

The head of the Brotherhood is called the Alt-
knecht. He is chosen every year, but can be deposed at any time if he prove unworthy of his post.
It is his mission to watch over the other members,
keep order, and dictate punishments, but when he
is caught erring himself he incurs a double forfeit.
When a new Alt-knecht is about to be chosen, the
seven oldest brothers are proposed as candidates.
With money received from the treasurer, these
repair to the public-house, there to await the decision of the confraternity. The other members meanwhile proceed to vote, and when they have made
a decision, send a deputation of two brothers to
invite the candidates to come and learn the result.

Twice the deputation is carelessly dismissed,
the candidates affecting to feel no interest in the
matter : only when the ambassadors appear for the
third time, two glasses of wine are filled for them,
and they are desired to salute the new Alt-knecht.

The two emissaries then take place on either side
of the newly chosen leader, and drink his health
with the words, "Helf Gott, Alt-knecht."   They
then all proceed back to the assembly room, where
the senior candidate says—

"God be with you, brother : you have sent for
us ; what do you want ?"

long pilgrim robes, cockle-shells, and wide flapping hats, were among
the most conspicuous figures at the royal funeral last summer.

The eldest amongst the voters answers for the others—

" We have chosen N. N. for our Alt-knecht; the other six can sit down."

The lucky candidate is now expected to play the shamefaced modest *rôle*, and say—

" Look farther, brother; seek for a better one."

" We have already looked," is the answer.

" And is it in truth your will that I and no other should be your head ? "

" It is our will."

" And shall it then be so ? "

" It shall be so."

" And may it be so ? "

" It may be so."

" Then God help me to act righteously towards myself and you."

" God help you, Alt-knecht."

The senior brother then solemnly presents him to the assembly, saying—

" See, brothers, this is the Alt-knecht you have chosen for the coming year. He is bound to under-take all journeys on behalf of the affairs of the confraternity, he will preside at our meetings, superintend the maids at their spinning evenings, and will punish each one according to his deserts; but when he is himself at fault, he shall be doubly visited (punished) by us."

Six other brothers occupy different posts of authority under the Alt-knecht. The first in rank of these is the Gelassen Alt-knecht, who takes the place of the Alt-knecht when absent : he is likewise treasurer, and has the office of presenting newly chosen members to the pastor. Once or twice a-month there is a meeting of the Brotherhood, at which the affairs of the confraternity are discussed, and misdemeanours judged. In presiding at these meetings, the Alt-knecht has in his hand, as insignia of his office, a wooden platter, with which he strikes on the table whenever he wishes to call the brothers to order.

Whoever, on these occasions, freely accuses himself of his faults, incurs only half the penalty ; but I am told that this contingency rarely occurs. The finable offences are numerous, and are taxed at six, ten, twenty kreutzers and upwards, according to the heinousness of the offence. Here are some of the principal delinquencies subject to penalties :—

1. Carelessness or slovenliness of attire—every missing button having a fine attached to it.

2. Bad manners at table, putting the elbows on the board, or striking it with the fist when excited.

3. Irregularity in church attendance, falling asleep during the sermon, yawning, stretching, &c., a particularly heavy fine being put upon snoring.

4. Having, on fast days, whistled loudly in the
street, or worn coloured ribbons in the hat.

Whoever be discontented with the punishment
assigned to him, and forgets himself so far as to
grumble audibly, incurs a double fine.

Four times yearly, before the Sacrament is administered in church, the Brotherhood hold what
they call their Versöhnungs-Abend (reconciliation
evening), at which they mutually ask pardon for
the injuries done.

Eight days after Quasimodo Sunday, the Alt-
knecht sends round an invitation to all newly con-
firmed youths to enter the confraternity. Their
incorporation is accompanied by various ceremonies,
one of which is that each newly chosen member is
laden with a burden of heavy stones, old rusty pots
and pans, broomsticks, and suchlike rubbish, secured round his neck by means of ropes — this
somewhat obscure ceremony being supposed to
signify the subjection of the new member to the
rules of the Brotherhood.

On his marriage a man ceases to be a member of
the Brotherhood, on leaving which, both he and
his bride must pay certain taxes in meat, bread,
and wine. Henceforth he belongs to the *Nachbar-
schaft* or neighbourhood. Every village is divided
into four neighbourhoods, each governed by a head
called the Nachbarvater. This second confrater-

nity is conducted in much the same manner as the Brotherhood, with the difference that its regulations apply to the reciprocal assistance which neighbours are bound to render each other in various household and domestic contingencies. Thus a man is only obliged to assist those who belong to his own quarter in building a house, cleaning out wells, extinguishing fires, and suchlike. He must also contribute provisions on christening, marriage, and funeral occasions occurring within his neighbourhood, and lend plates and jugs for the same.

The Nachbarvater has the responsibility of watching over the order and discipline in his quarter, enforcing the regulations issued by the pastor or the village *maire* or *Hann*, and assuring himself of the cleanliness of those streets which lie under his jurisdiction. When an ox or calf has perished through any accident, it is his duty to have the fact proclaimed in the neighbourhood, each family in which is then obliged to purchase a certain portion of the meat at the price fixed by the Nachbarvater, in order to lighten the loss to the afflicted family. His authority extends even to the interior of each household, and he is bound to report to the pastor the names of those who absent themselves from church. He must fine the men who have neglected to approach the Sacrament, as well as the women who have lingered outside the church wasting their time in senseless gossip. Children who have been overheard speaking disrespectfully of their parents ; couples whose connubial quarrels are audible in the street ; dogs wantonly beaten by their masters; vain young matrons who have exceeded the prescribed number of glittering pins in their head-dress, or girls surpassing their proper allowance of ribbons—all come under his jurisdiction ; and the Nachbarvater is himself subject to punishment if he neglect to report a culprit, or show himself too lenient in the dictation of punishment.

Of the third confraternity, to which belong the girls—viz., the *Schwesterschaft* or Sisterhood— there is comparatively little to say ; but the description of one of these Saxon village communities would not be complete without mention of the *Hann*, who, after the parson, is the most important man in the village.

The designation *Hann* has been derived by etymologists from the Saxon word *chunna* (hundred), out of which successively Hunna, Hund, Hunne, Honne, and Hann have been made. A Hundding or Huntari was a district comprising a hundred divisions (but whether heads of families or villages is impossible now to ascertain), and the Hund, Honne, or Hann was the title given to the man who governed this district. The appellation

Hann is to be found in documents of the fifteenth century in the Rhine provinces, but seems to have disappeared there from use since that time.

The Saxon village Hann is chosen every three years, and though but a peasant himself like the neighbours around, he becomes, from the moment when he is invested in " a little brief authority," an influential personage, whose word none dare to question. He is forthwith spoken of as the " Herr Hann," his wife becomes the " Frau Hanim," and *euer Weisheit* (your wisdom) is henceforth the correct formula of address.

In one village it is customary for the newly elected Hann to be placed on a harrow (the points turned upwards), and thus drawn in triumph round the village. The election takes place by votes, much in the same way as the nomination of a pastor, and with like circumspection. It is by no means easy to find a man well qualified for the office, for the Hann requires to have a very remarkable assortment of the choicest virtues in order to fit him for the place. He must be upright, honest, energetic, and practical, impervious to bribery, and absolutely impartial; moreover, he must not be poor, for *noblesse oblige*, and his new dignity brings many outlays in its train. The modest supply of crockery which has hitherto been ample for the requirements

of his family no longer suffices, for a Hann must
be prepared to receive guests; such luxuries as
coffee, loaf-sugar, and an occasional packet of cigars,
must now find their way into his house, to say

Saxon Peasant going to work.

nothing of paper, pens, and ink: who knows whether even a new table or an additional couple of
chairs may not become necessary?

Of course the Hann can only be chosen from

among those residing in the principal street, and it is considered to be rather an indignity if he has taken his wife from some side-street family—a disadvantage only to be condoned for by very exceptional merit on his own part.

It would be endless were I to attempt enumerating all the duties of a village Hann, so let it suffice to say that the whole responsibility of the arrangements for the health, security, cleanliness, and general welfare of the village rests upon his shoulders. School attendance, military conscription, and tax-collecting are but a few of the many duties which devolve on him. His it is to decide on what day the corn is to be cut or the hay brought home; through which street the buffaloes are to be driven to pasture, and at which fountain it is permitted for the women to wash their linen. He must assure himself that no cart return to the village after the curfew-bell has sounded; that the nightwatchmen—one in each neighbourhood—are punctual in going their rounds; and that the Nachbarväter make discreet and worthy use of their authority.

CHAPTER XII.

THE SAXONS: DRESS—SPINNING AND DANCING.

NOT without difficulty have these Saxons succeeded in keeping their national costume so rigidly intact, that the figures we meet to-day in every Saxon village differ but little from old bas-reliefs of the thirteenth and fourteenth centuries. Here, as elsewhere, even among these quiet, practical, prosaic, and unlovely people, the demon of vanity has been at work. Many severe punishments had to be prescribed, and much eloquence expended from the pulpit, in order to subdue the evil spirit of fashion which at various times threatened to spread over the land like a contagious illness. So in 1651 we find a whole set of dress regulations issued by the bishop for the diocese of Mediasch.

" 1. The men shall wear neither red, blue, nor yellow boots, nor shall the women venture to approach the Holy Sacrament or baptismal font in red shoes; and whoever conforms not to this regulation is to be refused admittance to church.

" 2. All imitation of the Hungarians' dress, such as their waistcoats, braids, galloons, &c., are prohibited to the men.

" 3. Be it likewise forbidden for men and for serving-men to wear their hair in a long foreign fashion hanging down behind, for that is a dishonour—for 'if a man have long hair, it is a shame unto him' (1 Cor. xi. 14).

" 4. The peasant folk shall wear no high boots and no large hats of wool, nor yet trimmed with marten fur, nor an embroidered belt, for he is a peasant. Who is seen wearing such will thereby expose himself to ridicule, and the boots shall be drawn off his legs, that he shall go barefoot.

" 5. The women shall avoid all that is superfluous in dress, nor shall they make horns upon their heads.[1] Rich veils shall only be worn by such as are entitled to them, neither shall any woman wear gold cords beneath her veil, not even if she be the wife of a gentleman.

" 6. Silk caps with golden stars are not suitable for every woman. More than two handsome jewelled pins shall no woman wear, and should a woman require more than two for fastening her veil, let her take small pins. Not every one's child is en-

[1] This would seem to be an allusion to the Roumanian fashion in some districts of twisting up the veil into a horn-like shape on the head.

titled to wear corals round its neck. Let no woman copy the dress of noble dames, for it is not suitable for us Saxons.

"7. Peasant maids shall wear no crooked (probably puffed) sleeves sewed with braids, for they have no right to them. They may wear no red shoes, and also on their best aprons may they have two braids only; one of these may be straight and the other nicked out, but neither over broad. Let none presume to wear high-heeled shoes, but let her conform to the prescribed measure under heavy penalty.

"8. Let the womenkind remember that such things as are forbidden become them but badly. Let them wear the *Borten*[1] according to the prescribed measurements. Let the *Herren Töchter* (gentlemen's daughters—meaning probably burghers) not make the use of gold braids over common, but content themselves with honourable fringes. The serving-girls shall go *absolutely* without fringes, nor may they buy silk cords of three yards length, else these will be taken from their head and nailed against the church wall.

"9. Among the women are beginning to creep in gold rings which cover the half finger *ad formam*

---

[1] The *Borten* is the high stiff head-dress worn by all Saxon girls, and which they only lay aside with their marriage.

et normam Nobilium—after the fashion of nobles; let these be *completely* forbidden."

The worthy prelate who issued all these stern injunctions appears to have been so uncommonly well versed in all the intricacies of female costume, as to make us wonder whether he had not missed his vocation as a man-milliner. It must have been a decidedly nervous matter for the women to attend service at his cathedral, with the consciousness that this terrible eagle-glance was taking stock of their clothes all the time, mentally appraising the value of each head-pin, and gauging the breadth of every ribbon. Most likely he succeeded in his object of keeping poor human vanity in check for a time, though not in rooting it out, for scarcely a hundred years later we find a new set of dress rules delivered from another pulpit :—

"First of all, it is herewith forbidden to both sexes to wear anything whatsoever which has not been manufactured in Transylvania. Furthermore, it is prohibited to the men—

" 1. To wear the so-called broad summer foreign hats.

" 2. The double-trimmed hats, with head of outlandish cloth,—only the jurymen and officials are allowed to wear them.

" 3. Trousers of outlandish cloth, or trimmed with braids.

"To the womankind let it be *completely* forbidden to wear—

" 1. Fine blue-dyed head-cloths.

" 2. White-starred caps.   Only the wives of officials and jurymen in the market towns may wear yellow-starred caps.

" 3. Silver head-pins costing more than two, or at the outside three, Hungarian florins.

" 4. Outlandish ribbons and fringes.

" 5. Borten (cap) 1 foot 8½ inches high, or lined inside with any material better than bombazine or glazed calico.

" 6. Neck-handkerchiefs.

" 7. All outlandish stuffs, linen, &c., &c."

Here follow several more regulations, concluding with the warning that whosoever dares to disregard them will be punished by having the said articles confiscated, besides paying a fine of from six to twelve florins Hungarian money, the offender being in some cases even liable to corporal punishment.

How strangely these old regulations now read in an age when lady's-maids are so often better dressed than their mistresses, and every scullion girl thinks herself ill-used if she may not deck herself out with ostrich-feathers of a Sunday!

A story which bears on this subject is told of Andrew Helling, a well-known and much-respected burgher of the town of Reps, about the beginning

of last century.   He was repeatedly chosen as
judge and burgomaster in his native place, and had
a daughter celebrated for her beauty who was engaged to be married.   On the wedding morning
the girl had been decked out by her friends in her
best, with many glittering ornaments and long
hanging ribbons in her headgear.   But what pleased
the young bride most was the bright silken apron,
a present from her bridegroom received that same
morning.   Thus attired, before proceeding to church
she repaired to her father to ask his blessing, and
thank him for all the care bestowed on her; and he,
well pleased with and proud of his beautiful child,
gazed at her with tenderly approving eye.   But of a
sudden his expression grew stern, and pointing to
the silken apron, he broke out into a storm of bitter
reproaches at her vanity for thus attiring herself in
gear only suitable for the daughter of a prince.
Hearing which, the bridegroom, aggrieved at the
dishonour shown to his gift, gave his arm to his
bride, and dispensing with the incensed father's
blessing, led her off to church.

Most likely, too, it was the desire to repress
all extravagance in dress which shaped itself into
the following prophecy, still prevalent throughout
Transylvania :—

"When luxury and extravagance have so spread
over the face of the earth that every one walks

about in silken attire, and when sin is no longer shame, then, say the Saxons, the end of the world is not far off. There will come then an extraordinary fruitful year, and the ripening corn will stand so high that horse and rider will disappear in it; but no one will be there to cut and garner this corn, for a dreadful war will break out, in which all monarchs will fight against each other, and the war-horse will run up to its fetlocks in blood, with saddle beneath the belly, all the way from Kronstadt to Broos without drawing breath. At last, however, will come from the East a mighty king, who will restore peace to the world. But few men will then remain alive in Transylvania—not more than can find place in the shade of a big oak-tree."

However, not all the authority of stern fathers and eloquent preachers was able to preserve the old costume intact in the towns, where little by little it dropped into disuse, being but seldom seen after the beginning of this century. What costumes there remain, are now locked away in dark presses, only to see the light of day at costumed processions or fancy balls, while many of the accompanying ornaments have found their way into jewellers' show-windows or museums. Only in the villages the details of dress are still as rigidly controlled as ever, and show no sign of degeneration just yet. Each village forming, as it does, a little colony by

itself, and being isolated from all outward influences, is enabled to retain its characteristics in a
manner impossible to the town.   No etiquette is
so rigid as Saxon village etiquette, and there are
countless little forms and observances which to
neglect or transgress would be here as grave as
it would be for a lady to go to court without
plumes in England, or to reverse the order of cham-
pagne and claret at a fashionable dinner-party.
The laws of exact precedence are here every whit
as clearly defined as among our upper ten thousand,
and the punctilio of a spinning-chamber quite as
formal as the ordering of her Majesty's drawing-
room.

These spinning meetings take place on winter
evenings, the young girls usually coming together
at different houses alternately, the young men
being permitted to visit them the while, provided
they do not interfere with the work.   There are
often two different spinning meetings in each village, the half-grown girls taking part in the one,
while the other assembles the full-fledged maidens
of marriageable age.   It is not allowed for any
man to enter a spinning-room in work-day attire,
but each must be carefully dressed in his Sunday's
clothes.   The eldest member of the Brotherhood
present keeps watch over the decorum of the
younger members, and assures himself that no

unbecoming liberties are taken with the other sex.

There is a whole code of penalties drawn up for those who presume to outstep the limits of proper familiarity, and the exact distance a youth is allowed to approach the spinning-wheel of any girl is in some villages regulated by inches. A fine of ten kreutzers is attached to the touching of a maiden's breast-pin, while stealing a kiss always proves a still more expensive amusement. As we see by ancient chronicles, these spinning meetings (which formerly used to be held in the towns as well) had sometimes to be prohibited by the clergy when threatening to degenerate into indecorous romps in any particular place ; but this custom, so deeply inrooted in Saxon village life, was always resumed after an interval, and, thanks to the vigilant watch kept up by the heads of the Brotherhood, it is seldom that anything really objectionable takes place. The men are allowed to join the girls in singing the Rockenlieder (spinning songs), of which there are a great number.

No man may accompany a girl to her home when the meeting breaks up, but each must go singly or along with her companions.

Many superstitions are attached to the spinning-wheel in Saxon households, besides the one which is mentioned in the chapter on weddings. So on

Saturday evening the work must be desisted with the first stroke of the evening bell, and there are many old pagan festivals which demand that the reel be spun empty the day before.

The girl who sits up spinning on Saturday night is considered as sinning against both sun and moon, and will only produce a coarse unequal thread, which refuses to let itself be bleached white. The woman who spins on Ash Wednesday will cause her pigs to suffer from worms throughout the year.

An amulet which preserves against accidents and brings luck in love matters may be produced by two young girls spinning a thread together in silence on St John's Day, after the evening bell has rung. It must be spun walking, one girl holding the distaff while the other twirls the thread, which is afterwards divided between the two. Each piece of this thread, if worn against the body, will bring luck to its wearer, but only so long as her companion likewise retains her portion of the charm.

For the twelve days following St Thomas (21st December) spinning is prohibited, and the young men visiting the spinning-room during that period have the right to break and burn all the distaffs they find; so it has become usual for the maidens to appear on the feast of St Thomas with a stick

dressed up with tow or wool to represent the distaff, in place of a real spinning-wheel.

The married women have also their own spinning
meetings, which are principally held in the six
weeks following Christmas ; and she is considered
to be a dilatory housewife who has not spun all
her flax by the first week in February. Sometimes
she receives a little covert assistance from her lord
and master, who, when he has no other work to do
in field or barn, may be seen half-shamefacedly
plying the distaff, like Hercules at the feet of
Omphale. On certain occasions the women hold
what they call *Gainzelnocht* (whole-night)—that is,
they sit up all through the long winter night,
spinning into the grey dawn of the morning.

Dancing takes place either at the village inn on
Sunday afternoons, or in summer in the open air,
in some roomy courtyard, or under a group of old
trees, the permission to dance having been each
time formally requested of the pastor by the head of
the Brotherhood. The Alt-knecht also sometimes
settles the couples beforehand, so as to ensure each
girl against the humiliating contingency of remaining partnerless, and no youth durst, under pain of
penalty, refuse the hand of any partner thus
assigned to him. Also each man can only stay near
his partner while the music is playing ; he may not

sit near or walk about with her during the pauses, but with the last note of the valse or *Ländler* he drops her like a hot potato, the girls retiring to one side of the room and the men remaining at the other, till the renewed strains of music permit the sexes again to mingle.

Only girls and youths take part in these village dances as a rule, though in some districts it is usual for young couples to dance for a period of six months after their marriage. Also there are some villages where the custom prevails of the married women dancing every fourth year, but more usually dancing ceases altogether with matrimony.

The usual dance which I have seen performed by Saxon peasants is a sort of valse executed with perfect propriety in a slow ponderous style, and absolutely unaccompanied by any expression of enjoyment on the part of the dancers. In some villages, however, the amusement seems to be of a livelier kind, for there I am told that certain dances require that the men should noisily slap the calves of their legs at particular parts of the music. A curious explanation is given of this. In olden times it seems their dress was somewhat different from what it is now. Instead of wearing high boots, they had shoes and short breeches; and as the stockings did not reach up to the knee, a naked strip of skin was visible between, as in the Styrian

and Tyrolese dress. In summer, therefore, when
dancing in a barn or in the open air, the dancers
were often sorely tormented by gnats and horse-
flies settling on the exposed parts; and seeking
occasional relief by vigorous slaps, these gradually
took the form of a regular rhythm which has survived the change of costume.

The music used on these occasions is mostly
execrable, both out of time and tune, unless indeed
they have been lucky enough to secure the services
of gipsy musicians; but this is rarely the case, for
bad as it is, the Saxon prefers his own music.

However, it is an interesting sight to look on at
one of these village dances, as the girls' costume is
both rich and quaint. Particularly interesting is
this sight at the village of Hammersdorf, whose inhabitants, as I before remarked, are celebrated for
their opulence. Only on the highest festivals,
three or four times a-year, is it customary for the
girls to don their richest attire for the dance, and
display all their ornaments—often an exceedingly
handsome show of jewellery, descended from mother
to daughter through many generations. Thus Pentecost, when there is dancing two days in succession in the open air, is a good time for assisting at
one of these rustic balls.

Each girl wears on her head the high stiff
Borten, which in shape resembles nothing so much

as a chimney-pot hat, without either crown or
brim, though this is perhaps rather an Irish way
of putting it. It is formed of pasteboard covered
with black velvet, and from it depend numerous
ribbons three or four fingers in breadth, hanging
down almost to the hem of the skirt. In some
villages these ribbons are blue, in others, as at
Hammersdorf, mostly scarlet and silver. The
skirt at Hammersdorf on Pentecost Monday was
of black stuff very full and wide, and above it a
large white muslin apron covered with embroidery,
with the name of the wearer introduced in the
pattern. The wide bulging black skirt was confined at the waist by a broad girdle of massive
gold braid set with round clumps of jewels at
regular intervals: these were sometimes garnets,
turquoises, pearls, or emeralds. Another ornament
is the *Patzel*, worn by some on the chest, as large
as a tea saucer, silver gilt, and likewise richly
encrusted with two or three sorts of gems: some
of these were of very beautiful and intricate work-
manship. Altogether, when thus seen collectively,
the costume presents a quaint and pretty appearance, with something martial about the general
effect, suggesting a troop of sturdy young Amazons,
—the silver and scarlet touches, relieving the simplicity of the black and white attire, being particularly effective.

On Pentecost Tuesday the dance was repeated, with the difference that this time all wore white muslin skirts and black silk aprons. None of them could tell me the reason of this precise ordering

Dressing for the Dance.

of the costume: it had always been so, they said, in their mothers' and grandmothers' time as well, to wear the black skirts on the Pentecost Monday and the white ones on the Tuesday.

Each girl carries in her hand a little nosegay of flowers, and has a large flowered silk handkerchief stuck in her waistband. Every youth is, of course, attired in his Sunday clothes ; and however hot the weather, it is *de rigueur* that he keep on the heavy cloth jacket during the first two dances. Only then, when the Alt-knecht gives the signal, is it allowed to lay aside the coat and dance in shirt sleeves, while the girls divest themselves of their uncomfortable head - dress — how uncomfortable being only too apparent from the dark red mark which it has left across the forehead of each wearer.

But if the young people are thus elegantly got up, the same cannot be said of their chaperons the mothers, who in their common week-day clothes have likewise come here to enjoy the fun. They have certainly made none of those concessions to society which reduce the lives of unfortunate dowagers to a perpetual martyrdom in the ball-room, but are as dirty and comfortable as though they were at home, each woman squatting on the low three-legged stool which she has brought with her.

The reason for this simplicity—not to say sloven-liness—of attire presently becomes obvious, as the lowing of kine and a cloud of dust in the distance announce the return of the herd, and in a body the

matrons rise and desert the festive scene, stool in
hand, for it is milking - time, and the buffaloes,
whose temper is proverbially short, durst not be
kept waiting : only when this important duty has
been accomplished do the mammas return to the
ball-room.

CHAPTER XIII.

THE SAXONS : BETROTHAL.

OATS have been defined by Dr Johnson as a grain
serving to nourish horses in England and men in
Scotland; and spite of this contemptuous definition, its name, to us Caledonian born, must always
awaken pleasant recollections of the porridge and
bannocks of our childhood. It is, however, a new
experience to find a country where this often un-
appreciated grain occupies a still prouder position,
and where its name is associated with memories
yet more pregnant and tender; for autumn, not
spring, is the season of Saxon love, and oats, not
myrtle, are here emblematic of courtship and betrothal.

In proportion as the waving surface of the green
oat-fields begins to assume a golden tint, so also
does curiosity awaken and gossip grow rife in the
village. Well-informed people may have hinted
before that such and such a youth had been seen

more than once stepping in at the gate of the big red house in the long street, and more than one chatterer had been ready to identify the speckled carnations which on Sundays adorned the hat of some youthful Conrad or Thomas, as having been grown in the garden of a certain Anna or Maria ; but after all, these had been but mere conjectures, for nothing positive can be known as yet, and ill-natured people were apt to console themselves with the reflection that St Catherine's day was yet a long way off, and that there is many a slip 'twixt cup and lip.

But now the great day which is to dispel all doubt and put an end to conjecture is approaching, —that day which will destroy so many illusions and fulfil so few ; for now the sun has given the final touch to the ripening grain, and soon the golden sheaves are lying piled together on the clean-shorn stubble field, only waiting to be carted away. Then one evening when the sun is sinking low on the horizon, and no breath of air is there to lift the white powdery dust from off the hedgerows, the sound of a drum is heard in the village street, and a voice proclaims aloud that "to-morrow the oats are to be fetched home ! "

Like wildfire the news has spread throughout the village : the cry is taken up and repeated with various intonations of hope, curiosity, anticipation, or triumph, "To-morrow the oats will be fetched!"

A stranger probably fails to perceive anything particularly thrilling about this intelligence, having no reason to suppose the garnering of oats to be in any way more interesting than the carting of potatoes or wheat; and, no doubt, to the majority of landowners the thought of to-morrow's work is chiefly connected with dry prosaic details, such as repairing the harness and oiling the cart-wheels. But there are others in the village on whom the announcement has had an electrifying effect, and for whom the words are synonymous with love and wedding-bells. Five or six of the young village swains, or maybe as many as eight or ten, spend that evening in a state of pleasurable bustle and excitement, busying themselves in cleaning and decking out the cart for the morrow, furbishing up the best harness, grooming the work-horses till their coats are made to shine like satin, and plaiting up their manes with bright-coloured ribbons.

Early next morning the sound of harness-bells and the loud cracking of whips cause all curious folk to rush to their doors; and as every one is curious, the whole population is soon assembled in the street to gaze at the sight of young Hans N., attired in his bravest clothes and wearing in his cap a monstrous bouquet, riding postilion fashion on the left-hand horse, and cracking his whip with ostentatious triumph, while behind, on the gaily decorated cart, is seated a blushing maiden, who lowers her eyes in confusion at thus seeing herself the object of general attention—at least this is what she is supposed to do, for every well-brought-up girl ought surely to blush and hang her head in graceful embarrassment when she first appears in the character of a bride; and although no formal proposal has yet taken place, by consenting to assist the young man to bring in his oats, she has virtually confessed her willingness to become his wife.

Her appearance on this occasion will doubtless cause much envy and disappointment among her less fortunate companions, who gaze out furtively through the chinks of the wooden boarding at the spectacle of a triumph they had perhaps hoped for themselves. " So it is the red-haired Susanna after all, and not the miller's Agnes, as every one made sure," the gossips are saying. " And who has young Martin got on his cart, I wonder? ˙ May I never spin flax again if it is not that saucy wench, the black-eyed Lisi, who was all but promised to small-pox Peter of the green corner house,"—and so on, and so on, in endless variety, as the decorated carts go by in procession, each one giving rise to manifold remarks and comments, and not one of them failing to leave disappointment and heart-burning in its rear.

This custom of the maiden helping the young man to bring in his oats, and thereby signifying her willingness to marry him, is prevalent only in a certain district to the north of Transylvania called the *Haferland*, or country of oats—a broad expanse of country covered at harvest-time by a billowy sea of golden grain, the whole fortune of the land-owners. In other parts, various other betrothal customs are prevalent, as for instance in Neppen-dorf, a large village close to Hermanstadt, inhabited partly by Saxons, partly by Austrians, or Ländlers, as they call themselves. This latter race is of far more recent introduction in the country than the Saxons, having only come hither last century in the time of Maria Theresa, who had summoned them to replenish some of the Saxon colonies in danger of becoming extinct. If it is strange to note how rigidly the Saxons have kept themselves from mingling with the surrounding Magyars and Roumanians, it is yet more curious to see how these two German races have existed side by side for over a hundred years without amalgamating,— and this for no sort of antagonistic reason, for they live together in perfect harmony, attending the same church, and conforming to the same regulations, but each people preserving its own individual costume and customs. The Saxons and the Ländlers have each their different parts of the church assigned to them : no Saxon woman would ever think of donning the fur cap of a Ländler matron, while as little would the latter exchange her tight-fitting fur coat for the wide hanging mantle worn by the other.

Until quite lately unions have very seldom taken place between members of these different races. Only within the last twenty years or so have some of the Saxon youths awoke to the consciousness that the Austrian girls make better and more active housewives than their own phlegmatic country-women, and have consequently sought them in marriage. Even then, when both parties are willing, many a projected union makes shipwreck upon the stiffneckedness of the two *paterfamilias*, who neither of them will concede anything to the other. Thus, for instance, when the Saxon father of the bridegroom demands that his future daughter-in-law should adopt Saxon attire when she becomes the wife of his son, the Ländler father will probably take offence and withdraw his consent at the last moment : not a cap nor a jacket, not even a pin or an inch of ribbon, will either of the two concede to the wishes of the young people. Thus many hopeful alliances are nipped in the bud, and those which

have been accomplished are almost invariably based
on the understanding that each party retains its own

Saxon betrothed couple.

attire, and that the daughters born of such union
follow the mother, the sons the father, in the matter of costume.

Among the Ländlers the marriage proposal takes place in a way which deserves to be mentioned. The youth who has secretly cast his eye on the girl he fain would make his wife prepares a new silver thaler (about 2s. 6d.) by winding round it a piece of bright-coloured ribbon, and wrapping the whole in a clean sheet of white letter-paper. With this coin in his pocket he repairs to the next village dance, and takes the opportunity of slipping it unobserved into the girl's hand while they are dancing. By no word or look does she betray any consciousness of his actions, and only when back at home she produces the gift, and acquaints her parents with what has taken place. A family council is then held as to the merits of the suitor, and the expediency of accepting or rejecting the proposal. Should the latter be decided upon, the maiden must take an early opportunity of intrusting the silver coin to a near relation of the young man, who in receiving it back is thereby informed that he has nothing further to hope in that direction; but if three days have elapsed without his thaler returning to him, he is entitled to regard this as encouragement, and may commence to visit in the house of his sweetheart on the footing of an official wooer.

In cases of rejection, it is considered a point of honour on the part of all concerned that no word should betray the state of the case to the outer world—a delicate reticence one is surprised to meet with in these simple people.

This giving of the silver coin is probably a remnant of the old custom of "buying the bride," and in many villages it is customary still to talk of the *Brautkaufen.*

In some places it is usual for the lad who is courting to adorn the window of his fair one with a flowering branch of hawthorn at Pentecost, and at Christmas to fasten a sprig of mistletoe or a fir-branch to the gable-end of her house.

To return, however, to the land of oats, where, after the harvest has been successfully garnered, the bridegroom proceeds to make fast the matter, or, in other words, officially to demand the girl's hand of her parents.

It is not consistent with village etiquette that the bridegroom *in spe* should apply directly to the father of his intended, but he must depute some near relation or intimate friend to bring forward his request. The girl's parents, on their side, likewise appoint a representative to transmit the answer. These two ambassadors are called the *Wortmacher* (word-makers)—sometimes also the *Hochzeitsväter* (wedding-fathers). Much talking and speechifying are required correctly to transact a wedding from beginning to end, and a fluent

and eloquent *Wortmacher* is a much-prized indi
vidual.

Each village has its own set formulas for each of
the like occasions—long-winded pompous speeches,
rigorously adhered to, and admitting neither of
alteration nor curtailment. The following fragment of one of these speeches will give a correct
notion of the general style of Saxon oration. It is
the *Hochzeitsvater* who, in the name of the young
man's parents, speaks as follows :—

" A good morning to you herewith, dear neighbours, and I further wish to hear that you have
rested softly this night, and been enabled to rise in
health and strength. And if such be the case, I
shall be rejoiced to hear the same, and shall thank
the Almighty for His mercies towards you ; and
should your health and the peace of your household not be as good as might be desired in every
respect, so at least will I thank the Almighty that
He has made your lot to be endurable, and beg
Him further in future only to send you so much
trouble and affliction as you are enabled patiently
to bear at a time.

" Furthermore, I crave your forgiveness that I
have made bold to enter your house thus early
this morning, and trust that my presence therein
may in no way inconvenience you, but that I may
always comport myself with honour and propriety,

so that you may in nowise be ashamed of me, and
that you may be pleased to listen to the few words
I have come hither to say.

"God the Almighty having instituted the holy
state of matrimony in order to provide for the
propagation of the human race, it is not unknown
to me, dearest neighbour, that many years ago you
were pleased to enter this holy state, taking to
yourself a beloved wife, with whom ever since you
have lived in peace and happiness; and that, furthermore, the Almighty, not wishing to leave you
alone in your union, was pleased to bless you, not
only with temporal goods and riches, but likewise
with numerous offspring, with dearly beloved children to be your joy and solace. And amongst
these beloved children is a daughter, who has pros-
pered and grown up in the fear of the Lord to be
a comely and virtuous maiden.

"And as likewise it may not be unknown to
you that years ago we too thought fit to enter
the holy state of matrimony, and that the Lord
was pleased to bless our union, not with temporal goods and riches, but with numerous offspring, with various beloved children, among whom
is a son, who has grown up, not in a garden of
roses, but in care and toil, and in the fear of the
Lord.

"And now this same son having grown to be a

man, has likewise bethought himself of entering
the holy state of matrimony; and he has prayed
the Lord to guide him wisely in his choice, and to
give him a virtuous and God-fearing companion.

"Therefore he has been led over mountains and
valleys, through forests and rivers, over rocks and
precipices, until he came to your house and cast
his eyes on the virtuous maiden your daughter.
And the Lord has been pleased to touch his heart
with a mighty love for her, so that he has been
moved to ask you to give her hand to him in holy
wedlock."

Probably the young couple have grown up in
sight of each other, the garden of the one father
very likely adjoining the pigsty of the other; but
the formula must be adhered to notwithstanding,
and neither rocks nor precipices omitted from the
programme : and even though the parents of the
bride be a byword in the village for their noisy
domestic quarrels, yet the little fiction of conjugal
happiness must be kept up all the same, with a
truly magnificent sacrifice of veracity to etiquette,
worthy of any Court journal discussing a royal
alliance.

And in point of fact a disinterested love-match
between Saxon peasants is about as rare a thing
as a genuine courtship between reigning princes.
Most often it is a simple business contract arranged

between the family heads, who each of them hopes to reap advantage from the bargain.

When the answer has been a consent, then the compact is sealed by a feast called the *Brautver-trinken* (drinking the bride), to which are invited only the nearest relations on either side, the places of honour at the head of the table being given to the two ambassadors who have transacted the business. A second banquet, of a more solemn nature, is held some four weeks later, when rings have been exchanged in presence of the pastor. The state of the weather at the moment the rings are exchanged is regarded as prophetic for the married life of the young couple, according as it may be fair or stormy.

Putting the ring on his bride's finger, the young man says—

"I give thee here my ring so true ;
God grant thou may it never rue !"

CHAPTER XIV.

THE SAXONS : MARRIAGE.

The 25th of November, feast of St Catherine,[1] is in many districts the day selected for tying all these matrimonial knots. When this is not the case, then the weddings take place in Carnival, oftenest in the week following the Sunday when the Gospel of the marriage at Cana has been read in church, and Wednesday is considered the most lucky day for the purpose.

The preparations for the great day occupy the best part of a week in every house which counts either a bride or bridegroom amongst its inmates. There are loaves and cakes of various sorts and shapes to be baked, fowls and pigs to be slaughtered : in wealthier houses even the sacrifice of a calf or an ox is considered necessary for the wedding feast; and when this is the case, the tongue is carefully

[1] St Catherine is throughout Germany the patroness of old maids —likewise in France, " coiffer la Sainte Catherine."

removed, and, placed upon the best china plate, with a few laurel leaves by way of decoration, is carried to the parsonage as the customary offering to the reverend Herr Vater.

The other needful provisions for the banquet are collected in the following simple manner. On the afternoon of the Sunday preceding the wedding, six young men belonging to the Brotherhood are despatched by the Alt-knecht from house to house, where, striking a resounding knock on each door, they make the village street re-echo with their cry, " Bringt Rahm ! " (bring cream). This is a summons which none may refuse, all those who belong to that neighbourhood being bound to send contributions in the shape of milk, cream, eggs, butter, lard, or bacon, to those wedding houses within their quarter ; and every gift, even the smallest one of a couple of eggs, is received with thanks, and the messenger rewarded by a glass of wine.

Next day the women of both families assemble to bake the wedding feast, the future mother-in-law of the bride keeping a sharp look-out on the girl, to note whether she acquits herself creditably of her household duties. This day is in fact a sort of final examination the bride has to pass through in order to prove herself worthy of her new dignity —so woe to the maiden who is dilatory in mixing the dough or awkward at kneading the loaves.

While this is going on, the young men have been to the forest to fetch firing wood—for it is a necessary condition that the wood for heating the oven where the wedding-loaves are baked should be brought in expressly for the occasion, even though there be small wood in plenty lying ready for use in the shed.

The cart is gaily decorated with flowers and streamers, and the wood brought home with much noise and merriment, much in the old English style of bringing in the Yule-log. On their return from the forest, the gate of the courtyard is found to be closed; or else a rope, from which are suspended straw bunches and bundles, is stretched across the entrance. The women now advance, with much clatter of pots and pans, and pretend to defend the yard against the besiegers; but the men tear down the rope, and drive in triumphantly, each one catching at a straw bundle in passing. Some of these are found to contain cakes or apples, others only broken crockery or eggshells.

The young men sit up late splitting the logs into suitable size for burning. Their duties further consist in lighting the fire, drawing water from the well, and putting it to boil on the hearth. Thus they work till into the small hours of the morning, now and then refreshing themselves with a hearty draught of home-made wine.

When all is prepared, it is then the turn of the
men to take some rest, and they wake the girls
with an old song running somewhat as follows :—

> " All in the early morning grey,
> A lass would rise at break of day.
>> Arise, arise,
>> Fair lass, arise,
>> And ope your eyes,
>> For darkness flies,
> And your true love he comes to-day.
>
> So, lassie, would you early fill
> Your pitcher at the running rill,
>> Awake, awake,
>> Fair maid, awake,
>> Your pitcher take,
>> For dawn doth break,
> And come to-day your true love will."

Another song of equally ancient origin is sung
the evening before the marriage, when the bride
takes leave of her friends and relations.[1]

> " I walked beside the old church wall ;
> My love stood there, but weeping all.
> I greeted her, and thus she spake :
> ' My heart is sore, dear love, alack !
>> I must depart, I must be gone ;
>> When to return, God knows alone !
>> When to return ?—when the black crow
>> Bears on his wing plumes white as snow.
>
> ' I set two roses in my father's land—
> O father, dearest father, give me once more thy hand !

[1] Out of the several slightly different versions of this song to be
found in different districts, I have selected those verses which
seemed most intelligible.

I set two roses in my mother's land—
O mother, dearest mother, give me again thy hand !
    I must depart, I must be gone;
    When to return, God knows alone !
    When to return ?—when the black crow
    Bears on his wing plumes white as snow.

'I set two roses in my brother's land—
O brother, dearest brother, give me again thy hand !
I set two roses in my sister's land—
O sister, dearest sister, give me again thy hand !
    I must away, I must be gone;
    When to return, God knows alone !
    When to return ?—when the black crow
    Bears on his wing plumes white as snow.

'I set again two roses under a bush of yew—
O comrades, dearest comrades, I say my last adieu !
No roses shall I set more in this my native land—
O parents, brother, sister, comrades, give me once more
    your hand !
    I must away, I must be gone;
    When to return, God knows alone !
    When to return ?—when the black crow
    Bears on his wing plumes white as snow.

'And when I came to the dark fir-tree,[1]
An iron kettle my father gave me;
And when I came unto the willow,
My mother gave a cap and a pillow.
    Woe's me ! 'tis only those who part
    Can tell how parting tears the heart !

'And when unto the bridge I came,
I turned me round and looked back again;
I saw no mother nor father more,
And I bitterly wept, for my heart was sore.
    Woe's me ! 'tis only those who part
    Can tell how parting tears the heart !

[1] Two fir-trees were often planted before Saxon peasant houses.

'And when I came before the gate,
The bolt was drawn, and I must wait;
And when I came to the wooden bench,
They said, "She's but a peevish wench!"
        Woe's me! 'tis only those who part
        Can tell how parting tears the heart!

'And when I came to the strangers' hearth,
They whispered, "She is little worth;"
And when I came before the bed,
I sighed, "Would I were yet a maid!"
        Woe's me! 'tis only those who part
        Can tell how parting tears the heart!

'My house is built of goodly stone,
But in its walls I feel so lone!
A mantle of finest cloth I wear,
But 'neath it an aching heart I bear.
Loud howls the wind, wild drives the snow,
Parting, oh, parting is bitterest woe!
On the belfry tower is a trumpet shrill,
But down the kirkyard the dead lie still.' "

Very precise are the formalities to be observed
in inviting the wedding-guests. A member of the
bride's family is deputed as *Einlader* (inviter), and,
invested with a brightly painted staff as insignia
of his office, he goes the round of the friends and
relations to be asked.

It is customary to invite all kinsfolk within the
sixth degree of relationship, though many of these
are not expected to comply with the summons, the
invitations in such cases being simply a matter of
form, politely tendered on the one side, and gra-
ciously received on the other, but not meant to be
taken literally, as being but honorary invitations.

Unless particular arrangements have been made
to the contrary, it is imperative that the invitations, in order to be valid, should be repeated with
all due formalities as often as three times, the
slightest divergence from this rule being severely
judged and commented upon, and mortal offence
has often been taken by a guest, who bitterly com-
plains that he was only twice invited. In some
villages it is, moreover, customary to invite anew
for each one of the separate meals which take place
during the three or four days of the wedding
festivities.

Early on the wedding morning the bridegroom
despatches his *Wortmann* with the *Morgengabe*
(morning gift) to the bride. This consists in a pair
of new shoes, to which are sometimes added other
small articles, such as handkerchiefs, ribbons, a cap,
apples, nuts, cakes, &c. An ancient superstition
requires that the young matron should carefully
treasure up these shoes if she would assure herself
of kind treatment on the part of her husband, who
" will not begin to beat her till the wedding-shoes
are worn out." The ambassador, in delivering over
the gifts to the *Wortmann* of the other party,
speaks as follows :—

" Good morning to you, Herr Wortmann, and to
all worthy friends here assembled : the friends on
our side have charged me to wish you all a very

good morning.   I have further come hither to
remind you of the laudable custom of our fathers
and grandfathers, who bethought themselves of presenting their brides with a small morning gift. So
in the same way our young master the bridegroom,
not wishing to neglect this goodly patriarchal custom, has likewise sent me here with a trifling
offering to his bride, trusting that this small gift
may be agreeable and pleasing to you."

The bride, on her side, sends to the bridegroom
a new linen shirt, spun, woven, sewed, and embroidered by her own hands. This shirt he wears
but twice,—once on his wedding-day for going to
church, the second time when he is carried to the
grave.

Before proceeding to church the men assemble
at the house of the bridegroom, and the women
at that of the bride. The young people only
accompany the bridal pair to church, the elder
members of both families remaining at home until
the third invitation has been delivered, after which
all proceed together to the house of the bride,
where the first day's festivities are held.

In some villages it is customary for the young
couple returning from church to the house of the
bridegroom to have their two right hands tied together before stepping over the threshold. A glass
of wine and a piece of bread are given to them ere

they enter, of which they must both partake together, the bridegroom then throwing the glass away over the house roof.

There is much speechifying and drinking of healths, and various meals are served up at intervals of three or four hours, each guest being provided with a covered jug, which must always be kept replenished with wine.

It is usual for each guest to bring a small gift as contribution to the newly set-up household of the young couple, and these are deposited on a table decked for the purpose in the centre of the courtyard, or, if the weather be unfavourable, inside the house—bride and bridegroom standing on either side to receive the gifts. First it is the bridegroom's father who, approaching the table, deposits thereon a new shining ploughshare, as symbol that his son must earn his bread by the sweat of his brow; then the mother advances with a new pillow adorned with bows of coloured ribbon, and silver headpins stuck at the four corners. These gay ornaments are meant to represent the pleasures and joys of matrimony, but two long streamers of black ribbon, which hang down to the ground on either side, are placed there likewise to remind the young couple of the crosses and misfortunes which must inevitably fall to their share. The other relations of the bridegroom follow in due precedence, each with a gift. Sometimes it is a piece of homespun linen, a coloured handkerchief, or some such article of dress or decoration; sometimes a roll of sheet-iron, a packet of nails, a knife and fork, or a farming or gardening implement, each one laying down his or her gift with the words, "May it be pleasing to you."

Then follow the kinsfolk of the bride with similar offerings, her father presenting her with a copper caldron or kettle, her mother with a second pillow decorated in the same manner as the first one.

Playful allusions are not unfrequently concealed in these gifts,—a doll's cradle, or a young puppy-dog wrapped in swaddling-clothes, often figuring among the presents ranged on the table.

Various games and dances fill up the pauses between the meals,—songs and speeches, often of a somewhat coarse and cynical nature, forming part of the usual programme. Among the games occasionally enacted at Saxon peasant weddings there is one which deserves a special mention, affording, as it does, a curious proof of the tenacity of old pagan rites and customs transmitted by verbal tradition from one generation to the other. This is the *Rössel-Tanz*, or dance of the horses, evidently founded on an ancient Scandinavian legend, to be found in Snorri's 'Edda.' In this tale the gods Thor and Loki came at nightfall to a peasant's house in a carriage drawn by two goats or rams, and asked for a night's lodging. Thor killed the two rams, and with the peasant and his family consumed the flesh for supper. The bones were then ordered to be thrown in a heap on to the hides of the animals; but one of the peasant's sons had, in eating, broken open a bone in order to suck the marrow within, and next morning, when the god commanded the goats to get up, one of them limped on the hind leg because of the broken bone, on seeing which Thor was in a great rage, and threatened to destroy the peasant and his whole family, but finally allowed himself to be pacified, and accepted the two sons as hostages.

In the peasant drama here alluded to, the gods Thor and Loki are replaced by a colonel and a lieutenant-colonel, while instead of two goats there are two horses and one goat; also the two sons of the peasant are here designated as Wallachians. Everything is, of course, much distorted and changed, but yet all the principal features of the drama are clearly to be recognised — the killing of the goat and its subsequent resurrection, the colonel's rage, and the transferment of the two Wallachians into his service, all being part of the performance.

At midnight, or sometimes later, when the guests

are about to depart, there prevails in some villages a custom which goes by the name of *den Borten abtanzen*, dancing down the bride's crown. This head-covering, which I have already described, is the sign of her maidenhood, which she must lay aside now that she has become a wife, and it is danced off in the following manner. All the married women present, except the very oldest and most decrepit, join hands—two of them, appointed as brideswomen, taking the bride between them. Thus forming a wide circle, they dance backwards and forwards round and round the room, sometimes forming a knot in the centre, sometimes far apart, till suddenly, either by accident or on purpose, the chain is broken through at one place, which is the signal for all to rush out into the courtyard, still holding hands. From some dark corner there now springs unexpectedly a stealthy robber, one of the bridesmen, who has been lying there in ambush to rob the bride of her crown. Sometimes she is defended by two brothers or relations, who, dealing out blows with twisted up handkerchiefs or towels, endeavour to keep the thief at a distance; but the struggle always ends with the loss of the head-dress, which the young matron bewails with many tears and sobs. The brideswomen now solemnly invest her with her new head-gear, which consists of a snowy cap and veil, held together by silver or jewelled pins, sometimes of considerable value. This head-dress, which fits close to the face, concealing all the hair, has a nun-like effect, but is not unbecoming to fresh young faces.

Sometimes after the bride is invested in her matronly head-gear, she, along with two other married women (in some villages old, in others young), is concealed behind a curtain or sheet, and the husband is made to guess which is his wife, all three trying to mislead him by grotesque gestures from beneath the sheet.

On the morning after the wedding, bridesmen and brideswomen early repair to the room of the newly married couple, presenting them with a cake in which hairs of cows and buffaloes, swine's bristles, feathers, and egg-shells are baked. Both husband and wife must at least swallow a bite of this unsavoury compound to ensure the welfare of cattle and poultry during their married life.[1]

After the morning meal the young wife goes to church to be blessed by the priest, escorted by the two brideswomen, walking one on either side. While she is praying within, her husband meanwhile waits at the church-door, but no sooner does

---

[1] So in the Altmark the newly married couple used to be served with a soup composed of cattle-fodder, hay, beans, oats, &c., to cause the farm animals to thrive.

she reappear at the threshold than the young
couple are surrounded by a group of masked
figures, who playfully endeavour to separate the
wife from her husband. If they succeed in so
doing, then he must win her back in a hand-to-
hand fight with his adversaries, or else give money
as ransom. It is considered a bad omen for the
married life of the young couple if they be sepa-
rated on this occasion; therefore the young husband takes his stand close against the church-door,
to be ready to clutch his wife as soon as she steps
outside—for greater precaution, often holding her
round the waist with both hands during the dance
which immediately ensues in front of the church,
and at which the newly married couple merely
assist as spectators.

As several couples are usually married at the
same time, it is customary for each separate wedding
party to bring its own band of music, and dance
thus independently of the others. On the occasion of a triple wedding I once witnessed, it was
very amusing to watch the three wedding-parties
coming down the street, each accelerating its pace
till it came to be a sort of race between them up
to the church-door, in order to secure the best
dancing place. The ground being rough and slant-
ing, there was only one spot where anything like
a flat dancing floor could be obtained; and the

winning party at once securing this enviable position, the others had to put up with an inclined
plane, with a few hillocks obstructing their ball-
room *parquet*.

The eight to ten couples belonging to each wedding-party are enclosed in a ring of bystanders,
each rival band of music playing away with heroic
disregard for the scorched ears of the audience.
" Walser ! " calls out the first group ; " Polka ! "
roars the second,—for it is a point of honour that
each party display a noble independence in taking
its own line of action ; and if, out of mere coinci-
dence, two of the bands happen to strike up the
self-same tune, one of them will be sure to change
abruptly to something totally different, as soon as
aware of the unfortunate mistake—the caterwaul-
ing effect produced by this system baffling all description. " This is nothing at all," said the Pastor,
from whose garden I was overlooking the scene,
laughing at the dismay with which I endeavoured
to stop my ears. " Sometimes we have eight or
ten weddings at a time, each with its own fiddlers
—that is something worth hearing indeed ! "

The rest of this second day is spent much in the
same way as the former one, only this time it is at
the house of the bridegroom's parents.

In some places it is usual on this day for the
young couple, accompanied by the wedding-party,

to drive back to the house of the bride's parents in order to fetch her *Truhe*—viz., the painted wooden coffer in which her trousseau has been stored. The young wife remains sitting on the cart, while her husband goes in and fetches the coffer. Then he returns once more, and addresses the following speech to his mother-in-law : " It is not unknown to me, dearest mother, that you have prepared various articles, at the toil of your hands, for your dearest child, for which may you be heartily thanked ; and may God in future continue to bless your labour, and give you health and strength to accomplish the same.

" But as it has become known to me that the coffer containing your dear child's effects has got a lock, and as to every lock there must needs be a key, so have I come to beg you to give me this key, in order that we may be enabled to take what we require from out the coffer." [1]

Among the customs attached to this first day of wedded life is that of breaking the distaff. If the young matron can succeed in doing so at one stroke across her knee, she will be sure to have strong and healthy sons born of her wedlock ; if not, then she has but girls to expect.

---

[1] In Sweden the mother takes her seat on the coffer containing her daughter's effects, and refuses to part with it till the son-in-law has ransomed it with money.

The third day is called the finishing-up day, each family assembling its own friends and relations to consume the provisions remaining over from the former banquets, and at the same time to wash up the cooking utensils and crockery, restoring whatever has been borrowed from neighbours in the shape of plates, jugs, &c., &c.—the newly married couple joining the entertainment, now at the one, now at the other house. This day is the close of the wedding festivities, which have kept both families in a state of bustle and turmoil for fully a week. Everything now returns to everyday order and regularity, the young couple usually taking up their abode in a small back-room of the house of the young man's parents, putting off till the following spring the important business of building their own house. Dancing and feasting are now at an end, and henceforth the earnest of life begins, though it is usual to say, that " only after they have licked a stone of salt together " can a proper understanding exist between husband and wife.

CHAPTER XV.

THE SAXONS : BIRTH AND INFANCY.

BY-AND-BY, when a few months have passed over the heads of the newly married couple, and the young matron becomes aware that the prophecies pointed at by the broken distaff and the doll's cradle are likely to come true, she is carefully instructed as to the conduct she must observe in order to ensure the wellbeing of herself and her child.

In the first place, she must never conceal her state nor deny it, when interrogated on the subject, for if she do so, her child will have difficulty in learning to speak; nor may she wear beads round her neck, for that would cause the infant to be strangled at its birth. Carrying peas or beans in her apron will produce malignant eruptions, and sweeping a chimney makes the child narrow-breasted.

On no account must she be suffered to pull off her husband's boots, nor to hand him a glowing

THE SAXONS : BIRTH AND INFANCY.   191

coal to light his pipe, both these actions entailing
misfortune. In driving to market she may not sit
with her back to the horses, nor ever drink at the
well out of a wooden bucket. Likewise her intercourse with the pigsty must be carefully regulated ; for should she, at any time, listen over attentively to the grunting of pigs, her child will have
a deep grunting voice ; and if she kick the swine
or push one of them away with her foot, the infant
will have bristly hair on its back. Hairs on the
face will be the result of beating a dog or cat, and
twins the consequence of eating double cherries or
sitting at the corner of the table.

During this time she may not stand godmother
to any other child, or else she will lose her own
baby, which will equally be sure to die if she walk
round a new-made grave.

If any one unexpectedly throw a flower at the
woman who expects to become a mother, and hit
her with it on the face, her child will have a mole
at the same place touched by the flower.

Should, however, the young matron imprudently
have neglected any of these rules, and have cause
to fear that an evil spell has been cast on her child,
she has several very efficacious recipes for undoing
the harm. Thus if she sit on the doorstep, with
her feet resting on a broom, for at least five minutes at a time, on several consecutive Fridays,

thinking the while of her unborn babe, it will be released from the impending doom; or else let her sit there on Sundays, when the bells are ringing, with her hair hanging unplaited down her back, or climb up the stair of the belfry tower and look down at the sinking sun.

When the moment of the birth is approaching, the windows must be carefully hung over with sheets or cloths, to prevent witches from entering; but all locks and bolts should, on the contrary, be opened, else the event will be retarded.

If the new-born infant be weakly, it is usual to put yolks of eggs, bran, sawdust, or a glass of old wine into its first bath.

Very important for the future luck and prosperity of the child is the day of the week and month on which it happens to have been born.

Sunday is, of course, the luckiest day, and twelve o'clock at noon, when the bells are ringing, the most favourable hour for beginning life.

Wednesday children are *Schlabberkinder*—that is, chatterboxes. Friday bairns are unfortunate, but in some districts those born on Saturday are considered yet more unlucky; while again, in other places Saturday's children are merely supposed to grow up dirty.

Whoever is born on a stormy night will die of a violent death.

The full or growing moon is favourable ; but the decreasing moon produces weakly, unhealthy babes.

All children born between Easter and Pentecost are more or less lucky, unless they happen to have come on one of the distinctly unlucky days, of which I here give a list :—

January 1st, 2d, 6th, 11th, 17th, 18th.
February 8th, 14th, 17th.
March 1st, 3d, 13th, 15th.
April 1st, 3d, 15th, 17th, 18th.
May 8th, 10th, 17th, 30th.
June 1st, 17th.
July 1st, 5th, 6th, 14th.
August 1st, 3d, 17th, 18th.
September 2d, 15th, 18th, 30th.
October 15th, 17th.
November, 1st, 7th, 11th.
December 1st, 6th, 11th, 15th.

I leave it to more penetrating spirits to decide whether these seemingly capricious figures are regulated on some occult cabalistic system, the secret workings of which have baffled my understanding, so that I am at a loss to explain why January and April have the greatest, June and October the least, proportion of unlucky days allotted to them ; and why the 1st and 17th of each month are mostly pernicious, while, barring the 30th of May and September, no date after the 18th is ever in bad odour.

Both mother and child must be carefully watched over during the first few days after the birth, and all evil influences averted. The visit of another woman who has herself a babe at the breast may deprive the young mother of her milk; and whosoever enters the house without sitting down, will assuredly carry off the infant's sleep.

If the child be subject to frequent and apparently groundless fits of crying, that is proof positive that it has been bewitched—either by some one whose eyebrows are grown together, and who consequently has the evil eye, or else by one of the invisible evil spirits whose power is great before the child has been taken to church. But even a person with quite insignificant eyebrows may convey injury by unduly praising the child's good looks, unless the mother recollect to spit on the ground as soon as the words are spoken.

Here are a few specimens of the recipes *en vogue* for counteracting such evil spells :—

" Place nine straws, which must be counted backwards from nine till one, in a jug of water drawn from the river *with* the current, not *against* it ; throw into the water some wood-parings from off the cradle, the doorstep, and the four corners of the room in which the child was born, and add nine pinches of ashes, likewise counted backwards. Boil up together, and pour into a large basin, leaving the pot upside down in it. If the boiling water draws itself up into the jug " (as of course it will), "that is proof positive that the child is bewitched. Now moisten the child's forehead with some of the water before it has time to cool, and give it (still counting backwards) nine drops to drink."

The child that has been bewitched may likewise be held above a red-hot ploughshare, on which a glass of wine has been poured ; or else a glass of water, in which a red-hot horse-shoe has been placed, given to drink in spoonfuls.

In every village there used to be (and may still occasionally be found) old women who made a regular and profitable trade out of preparing the water which is to undo such evil spells.

The Saxon mother is careful not to leave her child alone till it has been baptised, for fear of malignant spirits, who may steal it away, leaving an uncouth elf in its place. Whenever a child grows up clumsy and heavy, with large head, wide mouth, stump nose, and crooked legs, the gossips are ready to swear that it has been changed in the cradle—more especially if it prove awkward and slow in learning to speak. To guard against such an accident, it is recommended to mothers obliged to leave their infants alone, to place beneath the pillow either a prayer-book, a broom, a loaf of bread, or a knife stuck point upwards.

Very cruel remedies have sometimes been resorted to in order to force the evil spirits to restore the child they have stolen and take back their own changeling. For instance, the unfortunate little creature suspected of being an elf was beaten with a thorny branch until quite bloody, and then left sitting astride on a hedge for an hour. It was then supposed that the spirits would secretly bring back the stolen child.

The infant must not be suffered to look at itself in the glass till after the baptism, nor should it be held near an open window. A very efficacious preservative against all sorts of evil spells is to hang round the child's neck a little triangular bag stuffed with grains of incense, wormwood, and various aromatic herbs, and with an adder's head embroidered outside. A gold coin sewed into the cap is also much recommended.

Two godfathers and two godmothers are generally appointed at Saxon peasant christenings, and it is customary that the one couple should be old and the other young; but in no case should a husband and wife figure as godparents at the same baptism, but each one of the quartet must belong to a different family. This is the general custom, but in some districts the rule demands two godfathers and one godmother for a boy, two godmothers and one godfather for a girl.

If the parents have previously lost other children, then the infant should not be carried out by the door in going to church, but handed out by the window and brought back in the same way. It should be carried through the broadest street, never by narrow lanes or byways, else it will learn thieving.

The godparents must on no account look round on their way to church, and the first person met by the christening procession will decide the sex of the next child to be born—a boy if it be a man.

If two children are baptised out of the same water, one of them is sure to die; and if several boys are christened in succession in the same church without the line being broken by a girl, there will be war in the land as soon as they are grown up. Many girls christened in succession, denote fruitful vintages for the country when they have attained a marriageable age.

If the child sleep through the christening ceremony, it will be pious and good-tempered—but if it cries, bad-tempered or unlucky; therefore the first question asked by the parents on the party's return from church is generally, "Was it a quiet baptism?" and if such has not been the case, the sponsors are apt to conceal the truth.

In some places the christening procession returning to the house finds the door closed. After knocking for some time in vain, a voice from within summons the godfather to name seven bald men of the parish. This having been answered, a further question is asked as to the gospel read in church, and only on receiving this reply, " Let the little children come to me," is the door flung open, saying, " Come in ; you have hearkened attentively to the words of the Lord."

The sponsors next inquiring, " Where shall we put the child ? " receive this answer :—

> " On the bunker let it be,
> It will jump then like a flea.
> Put it next upon the hearth,
> Heavy gold it will be worth.
> On the floor then let it sleep,
> That it once may learn to sweep.
> On the table in a dish,
> Grow it will then like a fish."

After holding it successively in each of the places named, the baby is finally put back into the cradle, while the guests prepare to enjoy the *Tauf Schmaus*, or christening banquet, to which each person has been careful to bring a small contribution in the shape of eggs, bacon, fruit, or cakes ; the godparents do not fail to come each laden with a bottle of good wine, besides some other small gift for the child.

The feast is noisy and merry, and many are the games and jokes practised on these occasions. One of these, called the *Badspringen* (jumping the bath), consists in placing a washing trough or bath upside down on the ground with a lighted candle upon it.   All the young women present are then invited to jump over without upsetting or putting out the light.   Those successful in this evolution will be mothers of healthy boys.   If they are bashful and refuse to jump, or awkward enough to upset and put out the candle, they will be childless or have only girls.

The *Spiesstanz,* or spit dance, is also usual at christening feasts.   Two roasting-spits are laid on the ground cross-wise as in the sword dance, and the movements executed much in the same manner. Sometimes it is the grandfather of the new-born infant, who, proud of his agility, opens the performance singing :—

> " Purple plum so sweet,
> See my nimble feet,
> How I jump and slide,
> How I hop and glide.
> Look how well I dance,
> See how high I prance.
> Purple plum so sweet,
> See my nimble feet."

But if the grandfather be old and feeble, and the godfathers unwilling to exert themselves, then it is usually the midwife who, for a small consideration, undertakes the dancing.

It is not customary for the young mother to be seated at table along with the guests ; and even

though she be well and hearty enough to have
baked the cakes and milked the cows on that same
day, etiquette demands that she should play the
interesting invalid and lie abed till the feasting
is over.

Full four weeks after the birth of her child must
she stay at home, and durst not step over the
threshold of her courtyard, even though she has
resumed all her daily occupations within the first
week of the event. " I may not go outside till my
time is out; the Herr Vater would be sorely
angered if he saw me," is the answer I have often
received from a woman who declined to come out
on the road. Neither may she spin during these
four weeks, lest her child should suffer from
dizziness.

When the time of this enforced retirement has
elapsed, the young mother repairs to church to be
blessed by the pastor; but before so doing she is
careful to seek out the nearest well and throw
down a piece of bread into its depths, probably as
an offering to the *Brunnenfrau* who resides in
each water, and is fond of luring little children
down to her.

With these first four weeks the greatest perils of
infancy are considered to be at an end, but no
careful mother will fail to observe the many little
customs and regulations which alone will ensure

the further health and wellbeing of her child. Thus she will always remember that the baby may only be washed between sunrise and sunset, and that the bath water should not be poured out into the yard at a place where any one can step over it, which would entail death or sickness, or at the very least deprive the infant of its sleep.

Two children which cannot yet talk, must never be suffered to kiss each other, or both will be backward in speech.

A book laid under the child's pillow will make it an apt scholar; and the water in which a young puppy dog has been washed, if used for the bath, will cure all skin diseases.

Whoever steps over a child as it lies on the ground, will cause it to die within a month. Other prognostics of death are to rock an empty cradle, to make the baby dance in its bath, or to measure it with a yard measure before it can walk.

CHAPTER XVI.

THE SAXONS: DEATH AND BURIAL.

IN olden times, when the Almighty used still to
show Himself on earth, the people say that every
one knew beforehand exactly the day and hour of
his death.

Thus one day the Creator in the course of His
wanderings came across a peasant who was mending his garden paling in a careless, slovenly
manner.

"Why workest thou so carelessly?" asked the
Lord, and received this answer—

"Why should I make it any better? I have
only got one year left to live, and it will last till
then."

Hearing which, God grew angry and said—

"Henceforward no man shall know the day or
hour of his death; thou art the last one who has
known it." And since that time we are all kept
in ignorance of our death hour; therefore should

every man live as though he were to die in the
next hour, and work as if he were to live for
ever.

Death to the Saxon peasant appears in the light
of a treacherous enemy who must be met with
open resistance, and may either be conquered by
courageous opposition or conciliated with a bribe.
" He has put off death with a slice of bread," is
said of a man who has survived some great
danger.

When the first signs of an approaching illness
declare themselves in a man, all his friends are
strenuous in advising him to hold out against it,—
not to let himself go, but to grapple with this foe
which has seized him unawares. Even though all
the symptoms of typhus fever be already upon him,
though his head be burning like fire and his limbs
heavy as lead, he is yet exhorted to bear up against
it, and on no account to lie down, for that would
be a concession to the enemy.

In this way many a man goes about with death
upon his face, determined not to give in, till at
last he drops down senseless in the field or yard
where he has been working. Even then his family
are not disposed to let him rest. With well-meant
but mistaken kindness they endeavour to rouse
him by shouting in his ear. He must be made
to wake up and walk about, or it will be all over

with him; and not for the world would they send for a doctor, who can only be regarded as an omen of approaching death.[1]

Some old woman, versed in magic formulas and learned in the decoction of herbs and potions, is hastily summoned to the bedside, and the unfortunate man would probably be left to perish without intelligent advice, unless the pastor, hearing of his illness, takes upon himself to send for the nearest physician.

By the time the doctor arrives the illness has made rapid strides, and most likely the assistance comes too late. The first care of the doctor on entering the room will be to remove the warm fur cap and the heavy blankets, which are wellnigh stifling the patient, and order him to be undressed and comfortably laid in his bed. He prescribes cooling compresses and a medicine to be taken at regular intervals, but shakes his head and gives little hope of recovery.

Already this death is regarded as a settled thing in the village; for many of the gossips now re-

[1] On the rare occasions when the Saxon peasant consults a physician, he is determined to reap the utmost advantage from the situation. An amusing instance of this was related to me by a doctor to whom a peasant had come for the purpose of being bled. Deeming that the patient had lost sufficient blood, the doctor was about to close the wound, when the Saxon interposed. "Since I have come this long way to be bled, doctor," he remonstrated, "you might as well let ten kreutzers' worth more blood flow!"

member to have heard the owl shriek in the preceding night, or there has been an unusual howling of dogs just about midnight. Some remember how a flight of crows flew cawing over the village but yesterday, which means a death, for it is meat that the crows are crying for; or else the cock has been heard to crow after six in the evening; or the loaves were cracked in the oven on last baking day. Others call to mind how over-merry the old man had been four weeks ago, when his youngest grandchild was christened, and that is ever a sign of approaching decease. " And only a week ago," says another village authority, "when we buried old N—— N——, there was an amazing power of dust round the grave, and the Herr Vater sneezed twice during his sermon; and that, as every one knows, infallibly means another funeral before long. Mark my words—ere eight days have passed, he will be lying under the nettles!"

"So it is," chimes in another gossip. " He will hear the cuckoo cry no more."

The village carpenter, who has long been out of work, now hangs about the street in hopes of a job. "How is the old man?" he anxiously inquires of a neighbour.

"The preacher has just gone in to knock off the old sinner's irons," is the irreverent reply, at which the carpenter brightens up, hoping that he

may soon be called in to make the "fir-wood coat,"
for he has a heap of damaged boards lying by which
he fain would get rid of.

Sometimes, however, it is the thrifty peasant
himself, who, knowing the ways of village car-
penters, and foreseeing this inevitable contingency,
has taken care to provide himself with a well-made
solid coffin years before there was any probability
of its coming into use.   He has himself chosen out
the boards, tested their soundness, and driven a
hard bargain for his purchase, laying himself down
in the coffin to assure himself of the length being
sufficient.   For many years this useless piece of
furniture has been standing in the loft covered
with dust and cobwebs, and serving, perhaps, as a
receptacle for old iron or discarded boots; and now
it is the dying man himself who, during a passing
interval of consciousness, directs that his coffin
should be brought down and cleaned out — his
glassy eye recovering a momentary brightness as
he congratulates himself on his wise forethought.

Death is indeed approaching with rapid strides.
Only two spoonfuls of the prescribed medicine has
the patient swallowed.   "Take it away," he says,
when he has realised his situation—"take it away,
and keep it carefully for the next person who falls
ill.   It can do me no good, and it is a pity to waste
it on me, for I feel that my time has come.   Send

for the preacher, that I may make my peace with the Almighty."

The last dispositions as to house and property have been made in the presence of the pastor or preacher. The house and yard are to belong to the youngest son, as is the general custom among the Saxons; the eldest son or daughter is to be otherwise provided for. The small back-room belongs to the widow, as jointure lodging for the rest of her life; likewise a certain proportion of grain and fruit is assured to her. The exact spot of the grave is indicated, and two ducats are to be given to the Herr Vater if he will undertake to preach a handsome funeral oration, and to compose a suitable epitaph for the tombstone.

When it becomes evident that the last death-struggle is approaching, the mattress is withdrawn from under the dying man, for, as every one knows, he will expire more gently if laid upon straw.

Scarcely has the breath left his body than all the last clothes he has worn are taken off and given to a gipsy. The corpse, after being washed and shaved, is dressed in bridal attire—the self-same clothes once donned on the wedding morning long ago, and which ever since have been lying by, carefully folded and strewn with sprigs of lavender, in the large painted *Truhe* (bunker), waiting for the day when their turn must come round again. Pos-

sibly they now prove a somewhat tight fit; for the
man of sixty has considerably developed his proportions since he wore these same clothes forty
years ago, and no doubt it will be necessary to
make various slits in the garments in order to
enable them to fulfil their office.

The coffin is prepared to receive the body by a
sheet being spread over a layer of wood-shavings;
for the head, a little pillow, stuffed with dried flowers and aromatic herbs, which in most houses are
kept ready prepared for such contingencies. In
sewing this pillow, great care must be taken not
to make any knot upon the thread, which would
hinder the dead man from resting in his grave, and
likewise prevent his widow from marrying again;
also no one should be suffered to smell at the
funeral-wreaths, or else they will irretrievably lose
their sense of smell.

A new-dug grave should if possible not stand
open over-night, but only be dug on the day of the
funeral itself.

An hour before the funeral, the ringer begins to
toll the *Seelenpuls* (soul's pulse), as it is called;
but the sexton is careful to pause in the ringing
when the clock is about to strike, for "if the hour
should strike into the bell," another death will be
the consequence.

Standing before the open grave, the mourners

give vent to their grief, which, even when true and heartfelt, is often expressed with such quaint realism as to provoke a smile :—

"My dearest husband," wails a disconsolate widow, "why hast thou gone away? I had need of thee to look after the farm, and there was plenty room for thee at our fireside. My God, is it right of Thee to take my support away? On whom shall I now lean?"

The children near their dead mother—"Mother, mother, who will care for us now? Shall we live within strange doors?"

A mother bewailing her only son—"O God, Thou hast had no pity! Even the Emperor did not take my son away to be a soldier. Thou art less merciful than the Emperor!"

Another mother weeping over two dead children —"What a misfortune is mine, O God! If I had lost two young foals, at least their hides would have been left to me!" And the children, standing by the open grave of their father, cry out, "Oh, father, we shall never forget thee! Take our thanks for all the good thou hast done to us during thy lifetime, as well as for the earthly goods thou hast left behind"!

The banquet succeeding the obsequies is in some places still called the *Tor*—perhaps in reference to the old god Thor, who with his hammer presides alike over marriages and funerals.

CHAPTER XVII.

THE ROUMANIANS : THEIR ORIGIN.

"It is a fine country, but there are dreadfully many Roumanians," was the verdict of a respectable Saxon, who accompanied his words with a deep sigh and a mournful shake of the head. Evidently the worthy man thought necessary to adopt a deprecatory tone in alluding to these objectionable people, as though the presence of Roumanians in a landscape were matter for apology, like the admission of rats in a stable, or bugs in a bedstead. To an unprejudiced outsider, it is certainly somewhat amusing to observe the feelings with which the three principal races inhabiting this country regard each other : thus, to the Hungarian and the Saxon, the Roumanian is but simple unqualified vermin ; while the Saxon regards the Magyar as a barbarian, which compliment the latter returns by considering the Saxon a boor ; and the poor Roumanian, even while cringing before his Saxon and Roumanian masters, is taught by his religion to regard as unclean all those who stand outside his faith.

Briefly to sum up the respective merits of these three races, it may be allowable to define them as representing manhood in the past, present, and future tenses.

The Saxons *have been* men, and right good men too, in their day; but that day has gone by, and they are now rapidly degenerating into mere fossil antiquities, physically deteriorated from constant intermarriage, and morally opposed to any sort of progress involving amalgamation with the surrounding races.

The Hungarians *are* men in the full sense of the word, perhaps all the more so that they are a nation of soldiers rather than men of science and letters.

The Roumanians *will be* men a few generations hence, when they have had time to shake off the habits of slavery and have learned to recognise their own value. There is a wealth of unraised treasure, of abilities in the raw block, of uncultured talent, lying dormant in this ignorant peasantry, who seem but lately to have begun to understand that they need not always bend their neck beneath the yoke of other masters, nor are necessarily born to slavery and humiliation. In face of their rapidly increasing population, of the thirst for knowledge and the powerful spirit of progress which have arisen among them of late years, it is scarcely hazardous to prophesy that this people have a great future before them, and that a day will come when, other nations having degenerated and spent their strength, these descendants of the ancient Romans, rising phœnix-like from their ashes, will step forward with a whole fund of latent power and virgin material, to rule as masters where formerly they have crouched as slaves.

Two popular legends current in Transylvania may here find a place, as somewhat humorously defining the national characteristics of the three races just alluded to.

"When God had decreed to banish Adam and Eve from Paradise because they had sinned against His laws, He first deputed His Hungarian angel Gabor (Gabriel) to chase them out of the garden of Eden. But Adam and Eve were already wise, for they had eaten of the fruit of knowledge; so they resolved to conciliate the angel by putting good cheer before him, and inviting him to partake of it. In truth the angel ate and drank heartily of the good things on the table, and, after having eaten, he had not the heart to repay his kind hosts for their hospitality by chasing them out of Paradise, so he returned to heaven without having executed his commission, and begged the Lord

to send another in his place, for he could not
do it.

"Then God sent the Wallachian angel Florian,
thinking he was less fine-feeling and would execute
the mission better. Adam and Eve were sitting
at table when the servant of the Lord entered,
shod in leather *Opintschen* (sandals) and with fur
cap under his arm. After humbly saluting, he
told his errand. But Adam, on seeing the appearance of this messenger, felt no more fear, and
asked roughly, 'Hast brought no written warrant
with thee?' At this the angel Florian began to
tremble, turned round on the spot, and went back
to heaven.

"Then the Lord became angry, and sent down
the German Archangel Michael. Adam and Eve
were mightily terrified on seeing him, but resolved
to do their best to soften his heart; so they prepared for him a sumptuous meal of his favourite
dishes,—ham-sausage, pickled *Sauerkraut*, beer,
wine, and sweet mead. The German angel was
highly pleased, and played such a good knife and
fork that Adam and Eve began to feel light of
heart again. But hardly had the archangel eaten
his fill when, rising from the table, he swung his
flaming sword overhead and thundered forth to
his terrified hosts, 'Now pack yourselves off!' In
vain did our first parents beg and sue for mercy;

nothing served to touch the heart of the inflexible German angel, who, without further ado, drove them both out of Paradise."

The second legend relates to the Holy Sepulchre, and tells us how a deputation, consisting of a Hungarian, a Saxon, and a Wallachian, was once sent by the Transylvanian Diet to Palestine in order to recover the Saviour's body from the infidels. "They started on their journey full of hope, but when they had reached Jerusalem they found the sepulchre guarded by a strong enforcement of Roman soldiers. What was now to be done? was the question debated between them. The Hungarian was for cutting into the soldiers at once with his sword, but the canny Saxon held him back and said, 'They are stronger than we, and we might receive blows; let us rather attempt to barter.' The Wallachian only winked with one eye and whispered, 'Let us wait till nightfall, and then we can steal the body.'"

There has been of late years so much learned discussion about the origin of this Roumanian people, that it were presumption, in face of the erudite authorities enlisted on either side, to advance any independent opinion on the subject. German writers, especially Saxons, have been strenuous in sneering down all claims to Roman extraction, and

contending that whatever Roman elements remained over after their·evacuation of the territory,
must long since have been swallowed up in the
great rush of successive nations which passed over
the land in the early part of the middle ages.
Roumanian writers, on the contrary, are fond of
laying great stress on the direct Roman lineage
which it is their pride to believe in, sometimes,
however, injuring their own cause by over-anxiety
to claim too much,—laying too little stress on the
admixture of Slave blood, which is as surely a
fundamental ingredient of the race.   One of the
most enlightened Roumanian authors, Joan Slavici,
states the case more accurately in saying that the
ethnographical importance of the Roumanians does
not lie in the fact of their being descendants of the
ancient Romans, nor in that of the long-vanished
Dacien race having been Romanised by the con-
querors, but solely and entirely therein, that this
people, placed between two sharply contrasting
races, form an important connecting link in the
chain of European tribes.

The classical type of feature so often to be met
with among Roumanian peasants of both sexes,
pleads strongly in favour of the theory of Roman
origin ; and if in a former chapter I compared the
features of Saxon peasants to those of Noah's-ark
figures, rudely cut out of the very coarsest wood,

the Roumanians as often remind me of a type of face chiefly to be met with on cameo ornaments or ancient signet rings. If we take at random a score of individuals from any Roumanian village, we cannot fail to find goodly choice of classical profiles, worthy to be immortalised on agate, onyx, or jasper, like a handful of antique gems which have been strewn broadcast over the land.

Wallack, or Wlach, by which name this people was generally designated up to the year '48, points equally to Roman extraction—Wallack being but another version of the appellations Welsch, Welch, Wallon, &c., given by Germans to all people native of Italy. It may, however, not be superfluous here to mention, that at no period whatever did these people describe themselves otherwise than as " Romāns," Roumanians, and would have been as little likely to speak of themselves as Wallacks as would be an American to call himself a Yankee, or a Londoner to designate himself as a Cockney. As far as I can make out, a certain sense of opprobrium seems to be attached to this word Wallack as applied by strangers, explainable perhaps by the fact that the appellation Wlach was formerly used to describe all people subjugated by the Romans.

CHAPTER XVIII.

THE ROUMANIANS : THEIR RELIGION—POPES AND CHURCHES.

In order at all to understand the Roumanian peasant, we must first of all begin by understanding his religion, which alone gives us the clue to the curiously contrasting shades of his complicated character. Monsieur de Gerando, writing of the Wallacks some forty years ago, says—

" Aujourd'hui leur seul mobile est la religion, si on peut donner ce nom à l'ensemble de leurs pratiques superstitieuses ; " and another author, with equal accuracy, remarks that " the whole life of a Wallack is taken up in devising talismans against the devil."

Historians are very much divided as to the date of the Roumanians' conversion to Christianity, for while some consider this to have only taken place in the time of Patriarch Photius (in the ninth century), others are of opinion that they embraced

Christianity as early as the third century. It is not improbable that during the Roman occupation of Transylvania in the second and third centuries Christians may have come hither, and so imparted their religion to the ancient inhabitants with whom they intermingled.

Up to the end of the seventeenth century all the Transylvanian Roumanians belonged to the Greek Schismatic Church. In the year 1698, however, the Austrian Government succeeded in inducing a great portion of the people to embrace the Greek united faith, and acknowledge the supremacy of the Pope, and at the present day the numbers of the two confessions in Transylvania are pretty equally balanced, with only a small proportion in favour of the Schismatic Church.

The united Roumanians in Transylvania are subject to an archbishop residing at Blasendorf, while those of the Greek Schismatic Church stand under another archbishop, whose seat is at Hermanstadt.

Old chronicles of the thirteenth century make mention of the Wallacks as a people " which, though professing the Christian faith, is yet given to the practice of manifold pagan rites and customs wholly at variance with Christianity ; " and even to-day the Roumanians are best described by the paradoxical definition of Christian-pagans or pagan-Christians.

True, the Roumanian peasant will never fail to uncover his head whenever he passes by a wayside cross, but his salutation to the rising sun will be at least equally profound : and if he goes to church and abstains from work on the Lord's day, it is by no means certain whether he does not regard the Friday (Vinere), dedicated to Paraschiva (Venus), as the holier day of the two. The list of other unchristian feast-days is lengthy, and still lengthier that of Christian festivals, in whose celebration pagan rites may yet be traced.

Whoever buries his dead without placing a coin in the hand of the corpse is regarded as a pagan by the orthodox Roumanian. "*Nu-i-de-legea-noastra*" —he is not of our law—he says of such a one ; and whosoever stands outside the Roumanian religion, be he Christian, pagan, Jew, or Mohammedan, is invariably regarded as unclean, and consequently whatever comes in contact with any such individual is unclean likewise.

The Roumanian language has a special word to define this uncleanness—*spurcat*—which corresponds somewhat to the *koscher* and *unkoscher* of the Jews.

If any animal fall into a well of drinking water, then the well forthwith becomes *spurcat*, and *spurcat* likewise whoever drinks of this water. If it be a large animal, such as a calf or goat, which has fallen into the well, then the whole water must be baled out; and should this fail to satisfy the conscience of any ultra-orthodox proprietor, then the popa must be called in to read a mass over the spot where perhaps a donkey has found a watery grave. But when it is a man who has been drowned there, no further rehabilitation is possible for the unlucky well, which must therefore be filled up and discarded as quite too hopelessly *spurcat.*

Every orthodox Roumanian household possesses three different classes of cooking and eating utensils : unclean, clean for the meat days, and the cleanest of all for fast-days.

The cleansing of a vessel which has, through some accident, become *spurcat*, is only conceded in the case of very large and expensive articles, such as barrels and tubs; copious ablutions of holy water, besides thorough scouring, scraping, and rubbing, being resorted to in such cases. All other utensils which do not come under this denomination must simply be thrown away, or at best employed for feeding the domestic animals. The Roumanian who does not strictly observe all these regulations is himself *spurcat.*

This same measure he applies to all individuals whom he considers to be clean or unclean, according to their observance of these rules. The uncleanliness, according to him, does not lie in the individual, but in his laws which fail to enforce cleanliness ; the law it is, therefore, which is unclean, *lege spurcat*, which, for the Roumanian, is synonymous with unchristian. For instance, a man who eats horse-flesh is by him regarded as a pagan.

This recognition of the uncleanliness of most of his fellow-creatures is, however, wholly independent of either hatred or contempt on the part of the Roumanian, who, on the contrary, shows much interest in foreign countries and habits, and when he wishes to affirm the high character of a stranger, he says of him that he is a man who keeps his own law—*tine la legea lui*—spite of which the Roumanian will refuse to wear the coat or eat off the plate of this honourable stranger, and would regard any such familiarity as a deadly sin.

The idea so strongly rooted in the Roumanian mind, that they alone are Christians, and that, consequently, no man can be a Christian without being also a Roumanian, seems to imply that there was a time when the two words were identical for them, and that, surrounded for long by pagans with whom they could hold no sort of community, they lacked all knowledge of other existing Christian races.

On the other hand, these people are curiously liberal towards strangers in the matter of religion, allowing each one, whatsoever be his confession, to

enter their churches and receive their sacraments.
No Roumanian popa durst refuse to administer a
sacrament to whosoever may apply to him, be he
Catholic, Protestant, Jew, or pagan, provided he
submits to receive it in the manner prescribed by
the Oriental Church. So to-day, as 600 years ago,
the popa cannot, without incurring scandal, refuse
to bury a Jew, or administer the sacrament to a
dying infidel; his church must be open to all man-
kind, and all are welcome to avail themselves of its
blessings and privileges.

This liberality in religious matters cannot, however, be reversed, and no true Roumanian ever
consents to receive a sacrament from a priest of a
different confession; and though he may occasionally assist at a Protestant or Catholic service, he
conforms himself to no foreign forms of worship,
but is careful to comport himself precisely as though
he were in his own church. He does not mind
joining a Catholic procession on occasion, but no
power on earth can induce him to take part in a
strange funeral.

The position occupied by the Roumanian clergyman towards his flock is such a peculiar one, that
it deserves a special notice. Though his influence
over his people is unlimited, it is in nowise de-
pendent on his personal character. Unlike the

Saxon pastor, it is quite superfluous for the popa to present in his person a model of the virtues he is in the habit of describing from the altar. He may, for his part, be drunken, dishonest, and profligate to his heart's content, without thereby losing his prestige as spiritual head. Like the Indian Brahmins, his official character is absolutely intangible, and not to be shaken by any private misdemeanours; and the Roumanian proverb which says, "*face zice popa dar unce face el*"—that is to say, "do as the popa tells you, but do not act as he does"—describes his attitude with perfect accuracy. Only the popa has the privilege of wearing a beard, as he alone is privileged to indulge in certain pet vices which it is his mission officially to condemn, and, like the virtue of charity, this beard may often be said literally to cover a very great multitude of sins.

These Roumanian popas, with their thick curly beards, long flowing garments, and wide-brimmed hats, used to give me the impression of a set of jolly apostles, such as we sometimes see depicted on old church windows; not infrequently the extreme joviality of their appearance threatening to overpower the apostolic character altogether, and completing the simile by suggesting further ideas of glorious crimson sunsets deepening each tint of the mellow-stained glass.

Mr Boner, in his work on Transylvania, mentions an instance of a group of Roumanian villagers who were seen on a Saturday afternoon dragging their sorely resisting spiritual head in the direction of the church. On being asked what they were about, the peasants explained that they were going to lock him up till Sunday morning, else he would be too drunk to say mass for the congregation. "When church is over we shall let him out again." From personal observation, I have no doubt of the veracity of this story, having come across more than one Roumanian village popa who would have been none the worse for a little such judicious confinement.

Although of late years, thanks chiefly to the enlightened efforts of the late Archbishop Schaguna, much has been done to raise the moral standard of the Roumanian clergy, yet there remains still much to do before the prevailing coarseness, brutality, and ignorance too often characterising this class can be removed. At present the average village popa is simply a peasant with a beard, and is not necessarily a particularly respected or respectable individual. Many well-authenticated cases are told of popas who could not write or read, and who betrayed their ignorance by holding the book of Gospels upside down.

On week-days the popa goes about his agricul-

tural duties like any other peasant, digging in the
garden or going behind the plough as a matter of
course; his wife is a simple peasant woman, and
her children run about as dirty and unkempt as
any other brats in the village.

On one occasion when I had visited a Roumanian

Archbishop Schaguna.

church, I dropped twenty kreutzers (about fourpence)
into the hand of the peasant lass who had unlocked
the door for me. She accepted the coin with

226 THE LAND BEYOND THE FOREST.

humble gratitude, but I felt myself to have been guilty of a terrible *gaucherie* when I subsequently discovered the young lady to be no other than Madame Popa herself!

Towards any one of the higher classes the popa, as a rule, is crouching and obsequious, humbly uncovering his head, and hardly daring to take a seat when offered. An old Hungarian gentleman told me of a Roumanian popa who, when requested to be seated, declined so doing, as he considerately observed that he should not like to distress the noble gentleman by leaving vermin on his furniture.

The Roumanian churches offer a pleasant contrast to the bleak, uncompromising appearance of the Saxon ones. Even when architecturally not remarkable, they are invariably covered with a profusion of ornament and decoration of extremely artistic effect. Few places of worship appeal so strongly to the imagination as these oriental buildings, which, without as well as within, are one mass of warm soft colouring. The belfry tower is encircled by a procession of celestial beings, and the walls divided off into little arched niches beneath the roof, each of which harbours some quaint Byzantine saint, with pale golden aureole and shadowy palm-branch. Though the outlines may be somewhat

primitive, and the laws of perspective but imperfectly understood, nature, the greatest artist of all,
has here stepped in to complete the picture : summer showers and winter snows have mellowed each
tint, and blended together the colour into perfect
harmony.

The same style of ornament is repeated inside
with increased effect ; for here the saintly legions
which adorn the walls are brighter and more vivid,
stronger and fiercer looking, because in better preservation.   They seem to be the living originals of ·
which those others outside are but the pale ghosts,
and appear to rush at us from all sides as we enter
the place, increasing in numbers as our eyesight
gets used to the dim, mysterious twilight let in by
the narrow windows.   Not a corner but from which
starts up some grinning devil, not a nook but
reveals some choleric-looking saint, till we feel ourselves to be surrounded by a whole pageant of
celestial and diabolical beings, only distinguishable
from each other by the respective fashions of their
head-gear—horns or halos, as the case may be.

These horned devils play a very important part
in each Roumanian church, where usually a large
portion of the walls is given up to representations
of the place of eternal punishment.   The poor
Roumanian peasant, whose daily life is often so
wretched and struggling as hardly to deserve that

name, seems to derive considerable consolation from anticipations of the day when the tables are to be turned, and the hitherto despised poor shall receive an eternal crown. Thus the hapless victims depicted as being marched off to the infernal regions under the escort of several ferocious-looking demons armed with terrific pitchforks, are invariably recruited from the ranks of the upper ten thousand. They are all being conducted to their destination with due regard for etiquette, and rigid observance of the laws of exact precedence. First comes a row of kings, easily to be distinguished by their golden crowns; then a procession of mitred bishops, followed by a line of noblemen booted and spurred; while on the other side of the wall a crowd of simple peasants and a group of shaven friars are being warmly invited by St Peter, key in hand, to step over the threshold of the golden gate which leads to Paradise.

Each of these churches is divided into three sections: first, there is the sanctuary, partitioned off by trellised gates, painted and gilt, behind which the priest disappears at certain parts of the ceremony; then, in the body of the church, up to the step approaching the sanctuary, stand the men, and behind them, in a sort of outer department connected by an archway, are the women, next to the door, and close to the pictures of hell.

In the more primitive buildings there are rarely benches for the congregation, but a curious sort of prong may be sometimes seen, constructed out of the forked branch of a tree, and which, placed at intervals along the walls, is intended to give support to feeble old people unable to stand upright during a lengthy service.

It is a pretty sight to look on at the celebration of mass in any Roumanian church, more especially in summer, when every matron and maiden carries a bunch of sweet-scented flowers in her hand, and each man has a similar nosegay stuck in the cap which he holds beneath his arm. These flowers bestow an additional sprinkling of bright colour over the scene, and counteract any closeness in the atmosphere by their pungent aromatic scent.

CHAPTER XIX.

THE ROUMANIANS: THEIR CHARACTER.

THE Roumanian is very obstinate in character, and does not let himself be easily persuaded. He does nothing without reflection, and often he reflects so long that the time for action has passed. This slowness has become proverbial, for the Saxon says, "God grant me the enlightenment which the Roumanian always gets too late." In the same proportion as he is slow to make up his mind, he is also slow to change it. Frankness is not regarded as a virtue, and the Roumanian language has no word which directly expresses this quality. The Hungarians, on the contrary, regard frankness and truth-speaking as a duty, and are therefore often laughed at by their Roumanian neighbours, who consider as a fool any man who injures himself by speaking the truth.

Of pride the Roumanian has little idea as yet: he has been too long treated as a degraded and

serf-like being, and the only word approaching this
characteristic would rather seem to express the
vanity of a handsome man who sees himself ad-
mired.   Also for dignity the epithet is wanting,
and the nearest approach to it is to say that a man
is sensible and composed, if you would express that
he is dignified.

Revenge is cultivated as a virtue, and whoever
would be considered a respectable man must keep
in mind the injuries done to him, and show resentment thereof on fitting occasions.   Reconciliation
is regarded as opprobrious and forgiveness of
wrongs degrading.   But the Roumanian's rage is
stealthy and disguised, and while the Hungarian
lets his anger openly explode, the Roumanian will
dissemble and mutter between his teeth, " *Tine
mente*," " Thou shalt remember this ; " and his
memory is good, for he does not suffer himself to
forget.   When an injury has been done to him,
henceforward it becomes his sacred duty to brood
over his vengeance.   He must not say a good word
more to his enemy nor do him a service, and must
strive to injure his foe to the best of his ability—
with however this nice distinction, that he himself
do not profit by the injury done.   Thus, it would
not be consistent with the Roumanian's code of
honour were he to steal the horse or ox of his
enemy, but there can be no reasonable objection

to his advising or inducing another man to do so. Such behaviour is considered only right and just, and by so acting he will only be fulfilling his duty as an honest and honourable man.

The Roumanian does not seem to be courageous by nature—at least not as we understand courage —nor does courage exactly take rank as a virtue in his estimation, for courage implies a certain recklessness of consequences, and, according to his way of thinking, every action should be circumscribed, and only performed after due deliberation. When, however, driven to it by circumstances, and brought to recognise the necessity, he can fight bravely and is a good soldier. In the same way, he will never expose his life without necessity, and will coolly watch a house burning down without offering assistance ; but when compelled to action under military orders, he will go blindly into the fire, even knowing death to be inevitable.

What is commonly understood by military enthusiasm is wanting in the Roumanian (at least on this side of the frontier), for he is too ignorant to perceive the advantage of letting himself be shot in the service of a foreign master, for a cause of which he understands nothing and cares less. He is extremely sorry for himself when forced to enlist, and sometimes becomes most poetically

plaintive on the subject, as in the following verses
translated from a popular song :—

> " To the battle-field I go,
> There to fight the country's foe.
> Wash my linen, mother mine,
> All my linen white and fine.[1]
> Rinse it in thy tears, and then
> Dry on burning breast again.
> Send it, mother, to me there
> Where you hear the trumpet's blare.
> Where the banners droop o'erhead,
> There shall I be lying dead,
> Stricken by the musket's lead,
> Seamed by gashes rosy red,
> Trampled by the charger's tread."

Something of the spirit of the ancient Spartans
lies in the Roumanian's idea of virtue and vice.
Stealing and drunkenness are not considered to be
intrinsically wrong, only the publicity which may
attend these proceedings conveying any sense of
shame to the offender. Thus a man is not yet a
thief because he has stolen, and whoever becomes
accidentally aware of the theft should, if he have
no personal interest in the matter, hold his peace,
on the Shakespearian principle that

> " He that filches from me my good name
> Robs me of that which not enriches him,
> And makes me poor indeed."

Even the injured party whose property has been

---

[1] The Roumanian peasant has a passion for white snowy linen.
Usually it is his sweetheart on whom devolves the duty of keeping
it clean—or when he has no sweetheart, then his mother or sister.

abstracted, is advised if possible to reckon alone with the thief, without drawing general attention to his fault.

Neither is drunkenness necessarily degrading. On the contrary, every decent man should get drunk on suitable occasions, such as weddings, christenings, &c., and then go quietly to a barn or loft and sleep off his tipsiness. " *Bea cat vrei apoi te calcu si dormi*"—drink thy fill and then lie down and sleep—says their proverb; but any man who has been seen reeling drunk in the open street, hooted at by children and barked at by dogs, were it but once, is henceforward branded as a drunkard. It is therefore the duty of each Roumanian who sees a drunk man, to conduct him quietly to the nearest barn or loft.

There are some few villages where even the noblest inhabitants are not ashamed to be seen drunk in the open street, but in such villages the moral standard is a low one throughout.

Another curious side of the Roumanian's morality is the point of view from which he regards personal property, such as grain and fruit. In general, whatever grows plentifully in the fields, or, as they term it, "whatever God has given," may be taken with impunity by whoever passes that way, but with this restriction, that he merely take so much as he can consume at the moment. This is but right and just, and the proprietor who makes complaint at having his vineyard or his plum-trees rifled in this manner only exposes himself to ridicule. Whoever carries away of the fruits with him is a thief,—but, strictly speaking, only when he sells the stolen goods, not when he shares them quietly with his own family.

With regard to fowls, geese, lambs, and sucking-pigs, the rule is more or less the same. Whoever steals only in order to treat himself to a good dinner is not blamed, and may even boast of the feat on the sly ; but the man caught in the act is punished by having the stolen goods tied round his neck, and being led round the village to the sound of the drum to proclaim his shame to the people. If, however, he has stolen from a stranger—that is, some one of another village—the culprit does not usually lose his good reputation ; and he who robs a rich stranger is never considered base, but simply awkward to have exposed himself to the odium of discovery.

The Roumanian only looks at deeds and results, motives being absolutely indifferent to him. So the word passion he translates as *pâtima*, which really expresses weakness. Thus an *om pâtima*— a weak man—may be either a consumptive invalid, a love-sick youth, or a furious drunkard. Passion is a misfortune which should excite compassion, but not resentment; and whoever commits a bad action is above all foolish, because it is sure to be found out sooner or later.

An anecdote, which aptly characterises the Roumanian's moral sense, is told by Mr Patterson. Three peasants waylaid and murdered a traveller, dividing his spoils between them. Among his provisions they discovered a cold roast-fowl, which they did not eat. however, but gave to their dog, as, being a fast day, they feared to commit sin by tasting flesh. This was related by the murderers themselves, when caught and driven to confess the crime before justice.

While on the subject of fasts, I may as well here mention that those prescribed by the Greek Church are numerous and severe, and it is a well-ascertained fact that the largest average of crimes committed by Roumanians occurs during the seasons of Advent and Lent, when the people are in a feverish and over-excited state from the unnatural deprivation of food,—just as the Saxon peasants are most quarrelsome immediately after the vintage.

Another English traveller, speaking disparagingly of the serf-like crouching demeanour of the Roumanians, remarked that " perhaps nothing else could be expected of people who are required to fast 226 days in the year."

The inhabitants of each Roumanian village are divided into three classes :—

First, the distinguished villagers—front men— called *fruntasi* or *oameni de frunta*.

Second, the middle-men—*mylocasi* or *oameni de mana adona*—men of second-hand.

Third, the hind-men or *codas* (tail-men).

Each man, according to his family, personal gifts, reputation, and fortune, is ranged into one or other of these three classes, which have each their separate customs, rights, and privileges, which no member of another class durst infringe upon.

Thus the *codas* may do much which would not be suitable for the other two classes. The *mylocasi* have, on the whole, the most difficult position of the three, and are most severely judged, being alternately accused of presumption in imitating the behaviour of the *fruntas*, and blamed for demeaning themselves by copying the irregular habits of the *codas*. In short, it would seem to be all but impossible for an unfortunate middle-man to hit off the *juste milieu*, and succeed in combining in his person the precise proportions of dignity and deference required of his state.

Nor is the position of the front men entirely an easy one. Each one of these has a separate party of hangers-on, friends and admirers, who profess a blind faith and admiration for him—endorsing his

opinion on all occasions, and recognising his authority in matters of dispute. His dress, his words,
his actions are all strictly regulated on the axiom
noblesse oblige; but woe to him if he be caught
erring himself—for only in the case of the popa is
it allowable for the practice to differ from the
preaching. A *fruntas* may sit down to table with
the *codas* of his own village, whenever they are in
his service helping him to bring in the harvest or
to build a house; but he durst not, under pain of
losing caste, be equally familiar with any strange
codas.

There are, moreover, whole districts which are
reckoned as distinguished, and whose *codas* take
rank along with the *mylocasi,* or even the front men
of less aristocratic villages. A single woman, coming from one of these distinguished neighbourhoods,
may in a short time transform the whole village
into which she marries, the inhabitants eagerly
studying and imitating her dress, manners, and
gestures, down to the most insignificant details.

A distinctive quality of the Roumanian race is
the touching affection which mostly unites all members of one family. Unlike the Saxon who seeks
to limit the number of his offspring, the poor
Roumanian, even when plunged into the direst
poverty, yet regards each addition to his family

as another gift of God; while to be a childless wife is considered as the greatest of misfortunes.

Numerous instances are recorded of children of other nationalities, who, deserted by their unnatural parents, have been taken in by poor Roumanians, themselves already burdened with a numerous family.

There is an ancient Roumanian legend which tells us how in olden times there used to prevail the custom of killing off all old men and useless encumbrances, on the same principle as in Mr Trollope's 'Fixed Period.' One young man, however, being much attached to his parent, could not resign himself to executing this cruel order; but fearing the anger of his country-people, he concealed his father in an empty barrel in the cellar, where every day he secretly brought him food and drink.

But it came to pass that all arms-bearing men were summoned together to sally forth in quest of a terrible dragon which was devastating the land. The pious son, sorely puzzled to know how to provide his father with nourishment during his absence, carried together all the victuals in the house, lamenting to him that possibly he might never return from the expedition, in which case his beloved parent would be obliged to die of hunger. The old man answered—

" If in truth thou returnest not, then life has no more charms for me, and gladly will I let my weak body sink into the grave. But wouldst thou come back victorious out of the conflict with the dragon, listen to my words. The cavern inhabited by the monster has over a hundred subterraneous passages and galleries which run like a labyrinth in every direction, so that even if the enemy be killed, the victors, unable to find the outlet, will perish miserably. Therefore take with thee our black mare which goes to pasture with a foal, and lead them both to the mouth of the cavern. There kill and bury the foal, but take the mother with thee, and when the struggle with the dragon is over, she will safely lead thee back to the light of day."

The son then took leave of his father with many tears, and marched away with his comrades, and when he reached the cavern he obeyed the given directions, without, however, revealing the secret to any one.

After a desperate struggle, the monster in the cavern was slain; but terror and dismay took possession of the warriors when it proved impossible to find the outlet from this dreadful labyrinth. Then stepped forward the pious son with his black mare, and called upon the others to follow him. The mare began to neigh for her foal, and, seeking the daylight, soon hit on the right track, which brought them safely to the mouth of the cavern.

The warriors, seeing how their comrade had saved them all from certain death, now besought him to reveal to them how he chanced to have hit on this cunning device. But he now took fright that if he spoke the truth, not only his own life but that of his old father would be forfeited, for having thus dared to disobey the law of the land. Only at last, when all had sworn to do him no injury, did he consent to unseal his lips and tell them how, in his cellar, there lived his father, an old and experienced man, who, at parting, had given him this advice with regard to the mare.

On hearing this the warriors were mightily astonished, and one of them called out, " Our ancestor did not do wisely in teaching us to kill the old ones, for these are more experienced than we, and can often help the people with their sage counsels when mere strength of arm is powerless to conquer."

All applauded this sentiment, and the cruel law which demanded the death of the aged was henceforth abolished.

CHAPTER XX.

ROUMANIAN LIFE.

The Roumanians seem to be a long-lived race, and it is no uncommon thing to come across peasants of ninety and upwards, in full possession of all their faculties. In 1882 an old Roumanian peasant, being called as witness in a court of justice in Transylvania, and desired to state his age, was, like many people of his class, unable to name the year of his birth, and could only designate it approximately by saying, " I remember that, when I was a boy, our emperor was a woman," which, as Maria Theresa died in 1780, could not have made him much less than 110 years of age.

Many people have supposed the Roumanians to be more productive than other races, but the truth will more likely be found to be that, although the births are not more numerous than among many other races, the mortality among

infants is considerably less; the children inherit-
ing the hardy resisting nature of the parents, and,
so to say, coming into the world ready seasoned
to endure the hardships in store for them.

Perhaps it is because the Roumanian has himself so few wants that he feels no anxiety about
the future of his children, and therefore the
rapid increase of his family occasions him no
uneasiness. Having little personal property, he is
a stranger to the cares which accompany their
possession. Like the lilies of the field, he neither
sows nor reaps, and the whole programme of his
life, of an admirable simplicity, may be thus
summed up :—

In early infancy the Roumanian babe is treated
as a bundle, often packed in a little wooden oval
box, and slung on its mother's back, thus carried about wherever she goes. If to work in the
field, she attaches the box to the branch of a
tree; and, when sitting at market, it can be
stowed on the ground between a basket of eggs
and a pair of cackling fowls. When after a very
few months it outgrows the box, and crawls out
of its cocoon, the baby begins to share its parents' food, and soon learns to manage for itself.
The food of both children and adults chiefly consists of maize-corn flour, which, cooked with milk,
forms a sort of porridge called Balmosch, or if

boiled with water, becomes Mamaliga—first cousin to the polenta of the Italians. This latter preparation is eaten principally in Lent, when milk is prohibited altogether; and there are many families who, during the whole Lenten season, nourish themselves exclusively on dried beans.

When the Roumanian child has reached a reasonable age, it is old enough to be a help and comfort to its parents, and assist them in gaining an honest livelihood. By a reasonable age may be understood five or six, and an honest livelihood, translated — helping them to steal wood in the forest. Later on, the boy is often bound over as swine- or cow-herd to some Saxon landholder for a period of several years, on quitting whose service he is entitled to the gift of a calf or pig from the master he is leaving.

Once in actual possession of a calf, the Roumanian lad considers himself to be a made man. He has no ground of his own, but such petty considerations not affecting him, he proceeds to build himself a domicile wherever best suits his purpose, on some waste piece of land. Stone hardly ever enters into the fabrication of his building; the framework is roughly put together of wooden beams, and the walls clay-plastered and wattled, while the roof is covered with thatch of reeds or wooden shingles, according as he may happen to live nearest to a marsh or a forest. Yet, such as it is, the Roumanian's hut is his castle, and he is as proud of its possession as the king can be of his finest palace. Each man's hut is regarded as his own special sanctuary, and however intimate a man may be with his neighbour, it is not customary for him to step over the threshold, or even enter the courtyard, after dusk. Only in special and very pressing cases does this rule admit of any exception.

The inside of a Roumanian hut is by no means so miserable as its outward appearance would lead us to suppose. The walls are all hung with a profusion of holy pictures, mostly painted on glass and framed in wood ; while the furniture is brightly painted in rough but not inartistic designs—the passion these people have for ornamenting all their woodwork in this fashion leading them even to paint the yoke of their oxen and the handles of their tools. There is always a weaving-loom set up at one end of the room, and mostly a new-born baby swinging in a basket suspended from the rafters.

The produce of the loom, consisting in stuffs striped, chiefly blue, scarlet, and white, in oriental designs, sometimes with gold or silver threads introduced in the weaving, are hung upon ropes or displayed along the walls. These usually belong to the trousseau of the daughter (perhaps the self-same infant we see suspended from the ceiling), but can occasionally be purchased after a little bargaining.

Every Roumanian woman spins, dyes, and weaves as a matter of course ; and almost each village has its own set of colours and patterns, according to its particular costume, which varies with the different localities, though all partake alike of the same general character, which, in the case of the women, is chiefly represented by a long alb-like under-garment of linen reaching to the feet, and above two straight-cut Roman aprons front and back, which have the effect of a tunic slit up at the sides. The subject of Roumanian dress offers a most bewildering field for description, and the *nuances* and varieties to be found would lead one on *ad infinitum* were I to attempt to enumerate all those I have come across.

Thus in one village the costume is all black and white, the cut and make of an almost conventual simplicity, forming a *piquante* contrast to the blooming faces and seductive glances of the beautiful wearers, who thus give the impression of a band of light - hearted maidens masquerading in nun's attire. In other hamlets I have visited, blue or scarlet was the prevailing colour ; and a few steps over the Roumanian frontier will show us glittering costumes covered with embroidery and spangles, rich and gaudy as the attire of some oriental princess stepped straight out of the 'Arabian Nights.'

The Roman aprons, here called *câtrinte*, are in some districts—as, for instance, in the Banat—composed of long scarlet fringes, fully three-quarters of a yard in length, and depending from a very few inches of solid stuff at the top. The *résumé* of this attire — a linen shirt and a little fringe as sole covering for a full-grown woman — may, in theory, be startling to our English sense of propriety, but

Roumanian Costumes.

in practice the effect has nothing objectionable about it. Dress, after all, is merely a matter of comparison, as we are told by a witty French writer. A Wallachian woman considers herself fully dressed with a *chemise*, while a Hungarian thinks herself naked with only three skirts.

The head-dress varies much with the different districts : sometimes it is a brightly coloured shawl or handkerchief, oftener a creamy filmy veil, embroidered or spangled, and worn with ever varied effect; occasionally it is wound round the head turban fashion, now floating down the back like a Spanish mantilla, or coquettishly drawn forward and concealing the lower part of the face, or again twisted up in Satanella-like horns, which give the wearer a slightly demoniacal appearance.

Whatever is tight or strained-looking about the dress is considered unbeautiful : the folds must always flow downwards in soft easy lines, the sleeves should be full and bulging, and the skirt long enough to conceal the feet, so that in dancing only the toes are visible.

The men have also much variety in their dress for grand occasions, but for ordinary wear they confine themselves to a plain coarse linen shirt, which hangs down over the trousers like a workman's blouse, confined at the waist by a broad red or black leather belt, which contains various receptacles for holding money, pistols, knife and fork, &c. The trousers, which fit rather tightly to the leg, are in summer of linen, in winter of a coarse sort of white cloth. Of the same cloth is made the large overcoat which he wears in winter, sometimes replaced by a sheepskin pelisse.

ROUMANIAN WOMEN.

FROM A PHOTOGRAPH BY MADAME KAMILLA ASBOTH, HERMANSTADT.

Both sexes wear on the feet a sort of sandal called *Opintschen*, which consists of an oval-shaped piece of leather drawn together by leather thongs, beneath which the feet are swaddled in wrappings of linen or woollen rags.

Dress makes the man, according to the Roumanian's estimate, and rather than want for handsome clothes a man should deprive himself of food and drink. " *Stomacul nu are oglinda* "—the stomach has no mirror—says their proverb; therefore the man who has no fitting costume to wear on Easter Sunday should hide himself rather than appear at church shabbily attired.

To be consistent with the Roumanian's notion of cleanliness, his clothes should by rights be spun, woven, and made at home. Sometimes he may be obliged to purchase a cap or coat of a stranger, but in such cases he is careful to select a dealer of his own nationality.

Roumanian women are very industrious, and they make far better domestic servants than either Hungarians or Saxons, the Germans living in towns often selecting them in preference to their own countrywomen. In some places you never see a Roumanian woman without her distaff; she even takes it with her to market, and may frequently be seen trudging along the highroad twirling the spindle as she goes.

The men do not seem to share this love of labour, having, on the contrary, much of the Italian *lazzarone* in their composition, and not taking to any kind of manual labour unless driven to it by necessity. The life of a shepherd is the only calling which the Roumanian embraces *con amore*, and his love for his sheep may truly be likened to the Arab's love of his horse. A real Roumanian shepherd, bred and brought up to the life, has so completely identified himself with his calling, that everything about him—food and dress, mind and matter—has, so to say, become completely "sheepified." Sheep's milk and cheese (called *brindza*) form the staple of his nourishment. His dress consists principally of sheepskin, four sheep furnishing him with the cloak which lasts him through life, one new-born lamb giving him the cap he wears; and when he dies, the shepherd's grave is marked by a tuft of snowy wool attached to the wooden cross above the mound. His whole mental faculties are concentrated on the study of his sheep, and so sharpened have his perceptions become in this one respect, that he is able to divine and foretell to a nicety every change of the weather, merely from observing the demeanour of his flock.

Forests have no charm for the shepherd, who, regarding everything from a pastoral point of view, sees in each tree an insolent intruder depriving his

sheep of their rightful nourishment, and he covertly
seeks to increase his pasture by setting fire to the
woods, whenever he can hope to do so with impunity. Whole tracks of noble forest have thus been
laid waste, and it is much to be feared that half a
century hence the country will present a bleak and
desolate appearance, unless some means can be discovered in order to prevent this abuse.

CHAPTER XXI.

ROUMANIAN MARRIAGE AND MORALITY.

MARRIAGEABLE Roumanian girls often wear a head-dress richly embroidered with pearls and coins: this is a sign that their trousseaux are ready, and that they only wait for a suitor. The preparation of the trousseau, involving as it does much spinning, weaving, and embroidering, in order to get ready the requisite number of shirts, towels, pillow-covers, &c., considered indispensable, often keeps the girl and her family employed for years beforehand. In some districts we are told that it is customary for the young man who is seeking a girl in marriage to make straight for the painted wooden chest containing her dowry, and only when satisfied, by the appearance of the contents, of the skill and industry of his intended, does he proceed to the formal demand of her hand. If, on the contrary, the coffer prove to be ill-furnished, he is at liberty to beat a retreat, and back out of the affair.   The matter has been still further simplified in one village, for there, during the carnival time, the mother of each marriageable daughter is in the habit of organising a sort of standing exhibition of the maiden's effects in the dwelling-room, where each article is displayed to the best advantage, hung against the walls, or spread out upon the benches.   The would-be suitor is thus enabled to review the situation merely by pushing the door ajar, and need not even cross the threshold if the display falls short of his expectations.

In some districts a pretty little piece of acting is still kept up on the wedding morning.   The bridegroom, accompanied by his friends, arrives on horseback at full gallop before the house of his intended, and roughly calls upon the father to give him his daughter.   The old man denies having any daughter; but after some mock wrangling, he goes into the house, and leads out an old toothless hag, who is received with shouts and clamours.   Then after a little more fencing, he goes in again and leads out the true bride dressed in her best clothes, and with his blessing gives her over to the bridegroom.[1]

[1] In Sweden, when the guests sit down to the bridal banquet, an old woman decked in a wreath of birch bark, in which straw and goose-feathers are interwoven, and grotesquely dressed up with jingling harness, is led in and presented to the bridegroom as his consort,

An orthodox Roumanian wedding should last seven days and seven nights, neither less nor more; but as there are many who cannot afford this sacrifice of time, they circumvent the difficulty by interrupting the festivities after the first day, and resuming them on the seventh.

The ceremony itself is accomplished with much gaiety and rejoicing. The parents of the bridegroom go to fetch the bride, in a cart harnessed with four oxen whose horns are wreathed with flower garlands; the village musicians march in front, and the chest containing the trousseau is placed on the cart. One of the bride's relations carries her dowry tied up in a handkerchief attached to the point of a long pole.

Whoever is invited to a Roumanian wedding is expected to bring not only a cake and a bottle of wine, but also some other gift of less transitory nature—a piece of linen, an embroidered towel, a handkerchief, or suchlike.

In some villages it is customary for the bride, after the wedding feast, to step over the banqueting-table and upset a bucket of water placed there for the purpose.[1] After this begins the dancing, at which it is usual for each guest to take a turn while in a pompous speech her charms are expatiated upon. She is chased away with clamorous hooting, whereupon the bridesmen go out again, and after a mock search they lead in the bride.

[1] Supposed to denote fruitfulness.

with the bride, and receive from her a kiss in return for the civility.

An ancient custom, now fast dying out, was the
Tergul' de fete—the maidens' market—celebrated
each year at the top of the Gaina mountain, at a
height of nearly 6000 feet above the level of the
sea, and where all the marriageable girls for miles
around used to assemble to be courted on the 29th
of June, Feast of St Peter and St Paul. The trousseau, packed in a gaily decorated chest, was placed
in a cart harnessed with the finest horses or the
fattest oxen, and thus the girl and her whole family
proceeded to the place of rendezvous. Sheep,
calves, poultry, and even beehives, were likewise
brought by way of decoration ; and many people
went the length of borrowing strange cattle or
furniture, in order to cut a better figure and lure
on the suitors—although it was an understood thing
that only a part of what was thus displayed really
belonged to the maiden's dowry. The destination
being reached, each family having a girl to dispose
of erected its tent, with the objects grouped around,
and seated in front was the head of the family,
smoking his pipe and awaiting the suitors.

The young men on their side came also accompanied by their families, bringing part of their
property with them, notably a broad leather belt
well stocked with gold and silver coins.

When an agreement had been effected, then the betrothal took place on the spot, with music, dancing, and singing, and it hardly ever happened that a girl returned home unbetrothed from this meeting. But, to say the truth, this was, latterly, only because each girl attending the fair went there virtually betrothed to some youth with whom all the preliminaries of courtship had already been gone through, and this was merely the official way of celebrating the betrothal,—the Roumanians in these parts believing that good luck will only attend such couples as are affianced in this manner. Any girl who had not got a bridegroom *in spe* rarely went there at all, or, if she went, did not take her trousseau, but considered herself as a mere spectator.

In former days, however, this assemblage had a real signification, and was moreover dictated by a real necessity. There were fewer villages, and a far larger proportion than now of the population led the wandering nomadic life of mountain shepherds, cut off from intercourse with their fellow-creatures during the greater part of the year, and with no opportunity of making choice of a consort. The couples thus betrothed on the 29th of June could not be married till the following spring, for immediately after this date the shepherds remove their flocks to higher pasturages, and, proceeding southward as the year advances, do not re-

turn to that neighbourhood till the Feast of St
George.

Another curious custom in connection with the
maidens' market was, that on Holy Saturday each
girl who had been betrothed on the preceding 29th
of June on the Gaina mountain came to a village
of that district called Halmagy, dressed in her best
clothes, and there offered a kiss to each respectable
person of either sex she happened to meet on
her way. The individual thus saluted was bound
to give a present in return, even were it but a
copper coin, and to decline or resist the embrace
was regarded as the greatest affront. This custom, known as the kiss market, seems to have
originated at the time when all the newly married young shepherdesses used to leave the
neighbourhood to follow their husbands in their
roving life, and this was their mode of bidding
farewell to all friends and relations. This custom
has now likewise become almost extinct, for the
conditions of daily life have been considerably
modified during the last fifty years, and nowadays
the newly married shepherd, after a very brief
honeymoon, goes away alone with his flock, leaving
his wife established in the village, even though his
absence may extend over a year. Many Roumanian villages are thus virtually inhabited solely
by women, and to a population of several thou-

sand females we not unfrequently find but twenty
or thirty men, and these mostly old and decrepit,
the real lords and masters only appearing from
time to time on a short and flying visit.   Szeliste,
one of the largest Roumanian villages in the neighbourhood of Hermanstadt, and celebrated for the
good looks of its inhabitants, presents thus during
the greater part of the year, a touching array of
desolate Penelopes, and it is much to be feared
that the score of feeble old men left them as guar-
dians are altogether insufficient to defend the
wholesale amount of female virtue intrusted to
their charge.

The Roumanian always regards marriage with a
stranger as something opprobrious.   The man who
marries other than a Roumanian woman ceases to
be a Roumanian in his people's eyes, and is henceforward regarded as unclean; and a popa whose wife
was not a Roumanian would not be accepted by
any congregation.   Yet more severely condemned
is the woman who marries a stranger : the marriage itself is considered invalid, and no Roumanians who respect themselves would keep up
acquaintance with such a person.

According to their views, a girl should remain in her own village, but a man may, without
losing caste, marry into another neighbourhood.
Any father will consider it an honour to take a

strange son-in-law into his house, and the greater the distance this latter has come, in the same proportion does the honour increase. But a man who gives his daughter in marriage out of the village, loses his *prestige* in exact proportion as she goes farther away from home. "He has given his daughter away from home," is a reproach to which no man cares to expose himself.

In districts where Roumanians live together with other races professing the Greek faith, these marriage laws have been somewhat modified. So unions in the Bukowina with Ruthenians and in the Banat with Serbs, though still regarded as objectionable, are not so rare as they used to be.

No respectable girl should leave her parents' house unless driven to it by necessity; and if she be obliged to go into service, it should only be in the house of the popa, or in that of some particularly distinguished native of the place. The Roumanian girls serving in the towns are mostly such as have been obliged to leave their native village in consequence of a moral slip.

Much has been said about the lightness of behaviour characterising Roumanian girls—Saxons in particular being fond of drawing attention to the comparative statistics of the two races, which show, it is true, a very large balance of legitimate births

in their own favour.   If, however, we look at the
matter somewhat more closely, we are forced to
acknowledge that the words legitimate and illegitimate can only here be taken in a very modified
sense; for while the Saxon peasant marries and
divorces with such culpable lightness as to render
the marriage tie of little real value, the Roumanian
has introduced a sort of regularity even into his
irregular connections which goes far to excuse
them.   Whatever, also, may be said of the loose
conduct of many of the Roumanian married women,
the same reproach cannot be applied to the girls.

It happens frequently that among the Roumanians, who, like most Southern races, attain manhood
early, there are many young men who have chosen
a partner for life long before the time they are
called for military conscription; and as it is here
illegal for all such to marry before they have accomplished their three years' service as soldiers,
and no parents could therefore be induced to give
them their daughter, a curious sort of elopement
takes place.   Two or more of the lover's friends
carry off the girl, after a mock resistance on her
part, to some other village, where he himself awaits
her with his witnesses.   These latter receive the
reciprocal declaration of the young couple that
they wish to be man and wife.   The girl is then
solemnly invested with a head-kerchief, veil, or

comb, whichever happens to be the sign of matron-
hood in her village; and from that moment she
takes rank as a married woman, the lad as her
husband, and their children are considered as legitimate as those born in regular wedlock. Three or
four years later, when the young man has served
his time as a soldier, the union is formally blessed
by the priest in church; but in that case none of
the usual marriage festivities take place.

It is very rare that a man deserts the girl to
whom he has been wedded in this irregular fashion;
and in cases where he has been known to do so and
take another wife, both he and she are tabooed by
the neighbours, and the first wife is regarded as
the real one.

As, however, all children originating from such
unions are officially classified as illegitimate, the
barren figures would give an erroneously unfavourable idea of the Roumanian state of morality to
those unacquainted with these details; and it is
therefore really no anomaly to say that illegitimate
here is tantamount to three-quarters legitimate,
while the Saxons' legitimacy does not always quite
deserve that name.

A jilted lover will revenge himself on his mistress
by ostentatiously dancing with some other lass;
and in order to do her some material injury as
well, he goes secretly at night and cuts down

with a sickle the unripe hemp and flax which
were to have served for spinning her wedding
clothes.   It is always an understood thing that
the hemp belongs to the female members of the
family, and there is a certain poetry in the idea
of thus cutting off the faithless one's thread.
Thus the father, finding his hemp prematurely
cut down, is at once aware that something has
gone wrong about his daughter's love-affair.

CHAPTER XXII.

THE ROUMANIANS : DANCING, SONGS, MUSIC, STORIES, AND PROVERBS.

THE dances habitual among the Roumanians may briefly be divided into three sorts :—

1. *Caluseri* and *Batuta*, ancient traditional dances performed by men only, and often executed at fairs and public festivals. For these a fixed number of dancers is required, and a leader called the *Vatav*. Each dancer is provided with a long staff, which he occasionally strikes on the ground in time to the music.

2. *Hora* and *Breûl*, round dances executed either by both sexes or by men only.

3. *Ardeleana, Lugojana, Marnteana, Pe-picior*, and *Hategeana*, danced by both sexes together, and in which each man may have two or more female partners.

These last-named dances rather resemble a minuet or quadrille, and are chiefly made up of a sort of swaying, balancing movement, alternately advancing and retreating, with varied modes of expression and different rates of velocity. Thus the Ardeleana is slow, the Marnteana rather quicker but still dignified, and the Pe-picior is fastest of all. Also each separate dance has two distinct measures, as in the Scotch reel or the Hungarian *csardas*—the slow rhythm being called *domol*, or reflectively, and the fast one being danced *cu foc*, with fire.

All these dances are found in different districts with varied appellations.

There is also a very singular dance which I have not myself witnessed, but which is said to be sometimes performed in front of the church in order to ensure a good harvest—one necessary condition of which is that the people should dance till in a state of violent perspiration, figurative of the rain which is required to make the corn grow, then the arms must he held on high for the hops to grow, wild jumps in the air for the vines, and so on, each grain and fruit having a special movement attributed to it, the dance being kept up till the dancers have to give in from sheer fatigue.

The Roumanian does not say that a man is dancing with a girl, but that " he dances her," as you would talk of spinning a top. This conveys the right impression—namely, that the man directs her dancing and disposes her attitudes, so as to show off her grace and charms to the best advantage. Thus a good dancer here does not imply a man who dances well himself, but rather one skilful at showing off two or three partners at a time. He acts, in fact, as a sort of showman to the assortment of graces under his charge, to which he calls attention by appropriate rhymes and verses. Therefore the sharpest wit rather than the nimblest legs is required for the post of *Vatav flacailor*, or director of dances in the village.

Dancing usually takes place in the open air, and in villages where ball-room etiquette is duly observed the fair ones can only be conducted to the dance by the director himself, or by one of his appointed aides-de-camp. It is so arranged that after the leader has for a time shown off several girls in the manner described—so to say, set them agoing—he makes a sign to other young men to take them off his hands, while he himself repeats the proceeding with other *débutantes*.

The music usually consists of bagpipes and violin, the latter sometimes replaced by one or two flutes. The musicians, who are frequently blind men or cripples, stand in the centre, the dancers revolving around them. Tzigane players are rarely made use of for Roumanian dances, as they do not interpret the Roumanian music correctly, and are

accused of imparting a bold licentious character
to it.

There are many occasions on which music is
prescribed, and on all such it should not be wanting; but it is considered unseemly for music to
play without special motive, and when the Roumanian hears music he invariably asks, " La ce
cântà ? "—for whom do they play ?

Fully as many matrons as maidens figure at the
village merry-makings, for, unlike the Saxon, the
Roumanian woman does not dream of giving up
dancing at her marriage. Wedlock is to her an
emancipation, not a bondage, and she only begins
really to enjoy her life from the moment she becomes a wife. For instance, it is considered quite
correct for a married woman, especially if she has
got children, to suffer herself to be publicly kissed
and embraced by her dancer, and no one present
would think of taking umbrage at such harmless
liberties.

In reciting or making a speech, the Roumanian
is careful to speak slowly and distinctly, with
dignity and deliberation, and to avoid much ges-
ticulation, which is regarded as ridiculous. It
is also considered distinguished to speak rather
obscurely, and veil the meaning under figures of
speech,—a man who says his meaning plainly in

so many words being considered as wanting in breeding.

As in Italy, the *recitatore* (story-teller), called here *provestitore*, holds an important place among the Roumanians. The stories recited usually belong to the class of ogre and fairy tale, and would seem rather adapted to a nursery audience than to a circle of full-grown men and women. Sometimes in verse, sometimes in prose, these stories oftenest set forth the adventures of some prince subjected to the cruel persecutions of a giant or sorcerer. The hero has usually a series of tasks allotted to him, or difficulties to be overcome, before he is permitted to enjoy his father's throne in peace and lead home the beautiful princess to whom he is attached. The tasks dealt out to him must be three at least, sometimes also six, seven, nine, or twelve, but never more than this last number, which indeed is quite sufficient for the endurance even of a fairy prince. When the tasks are nine or twelve in number, they are then grouped together in batches of three, each batch being finished off with some stereotyped phrase, such as, "But our hero's trials were not yet over by any means, and much remains still to be told." As a matter of course, these trials must always be arranged *crescendo*, advancing in horror and difficulty towards the end.

The story invariably opens with the words—

" A fost ce a fost; dacà n'ar fi fost nici nu s'ar povesti," which, corresponding to our " once upon a time," may be thus translated—" It was what once took place, and if it had never been, it would not now be related ; " and the concluding phrase is often this one—" And if they have not died, they are all yet alive."

It is not every one who can relate a story correctly according to the Roumanian's mode of thinking. He is most particular as to the precise inflections of voice, which must alternately be slow and impressive, or impetuous and hurried, according to the requirements of the narrative. If the story winds up with a wedding, the narrator is careful to observe that he also was present on the occasion, in proof of which he enumerates at great length the names of the guests invited and the dishes which formed part of the banquet; and according to the fertility of imagination he displays in describing these details, he will be classed by his audience as a *provestitore* of first, second, or third rank.

The Roumanians have a vast *répertoire* of songs and rhymes for particular occasions, and many of these people seem to possess great natural fluency for expressing themselves in verse, assisted, no doubt, by the rich choice of rhymes offered by their language. Some people would seem to talk as

easily in verse as in prose, and there are districts
where it is not considered seemly to court a girl
otherwise than in rhymed speech. All these
rhymes, as well as most of their songs and ballads,
are moulded in verse four feet, which best adapts
itself to the fundamental measure of Roumanian
music. Among the principal forms of song prevalent in the country are the *Doina*, the *Ballad*,
the *Kolinda*, the *Cantece de Irogi*, the *Cantece de
Stea*, the *Plugul*, the *Cantece de Paparuga*, the
Cantece de Nunta, the *Descantece*, and the *Bocete*.

1. The *Doina* is a lyrical poem, mostly of a mournful monotonous character, much resembling the
gloomy *Dumkas* of the Rhuthenians, and from which,
perhaps, its name is derived ; and this is all the more
probable, as many of the songs sung by the Roumanians of the Bukowina are identical with those
to be heard sung by their countrymen living in the
Hungarian Banat. Thus it is of curious effect to
hear the celebrated song of the Dneister, " Nistrule
riu blestemal "—Dniester, cursed river—in which
lament is made over the women carried off by the
Tartars, sung on the plains of Hungary, so many
hundred miles away from the scenes which originated it.

2. The *Ballad*, also called *Cantece*, or song
proper, its title usually specifying whose particular
song it is : for instance, " Cantecul lui Horia "—the

song of Hora, or more literally, Hora his song—lui Jancu, lui Marko, &c.

These ballads are sung to the accompaniment of a shepherd's pipe or flute, but are oftener merely recited, it not being considered good form to have them sung except by blind or crippled beggars, such as go about at markets or fairs.[1]

3. The *Kolinda*, or Christmas song, the name derived from a heathen goddess, Lada.[2] These consist of songs and dialogues, oftenest of a mythological character, and bearing no sort of allusion to

[1] There is a story told of a village (but whether Hungarian or Roumanian I am unable to say) which, up to the year 1536, used to be inhabited by cripples, hunchbacks, lame, maimed, and blind men only, and which went by the name of the "Republic of Cripples." No well-grown and healthy persons were ever suffered to settle here, for fear of spoiling the deformity of their race ; and all new-born children unlucky enough to enter the world with normally organised frames were instantly mutilated.

The inhabitants of this village, turning these infirmities to account, made a play of wandering over the country begging and singing at all fairs and markets, and trading on the compassion excited by their wretched appearance. They had also their own language, called the language of the blind, and were in so far privileged above the useful and industrious citizens as to be exempted from all taxes.

[2] The Council of Constantinople, 869, forbade the members of the Oriental Church to keep the feast of the pagan goddess Kolinda, or Lada, occurring on the shortest day. These Kolinda songs appear to be of Slav origin, since we find the Koleda among the Bohemians, Serbs, and Slavonians, the Koleda among Poles, and the Kolad with the Russians. Yet further proof of this would seem to be that unmistakable resemblance to the Slav words *Kaulo*, *Kul*, *Kolo*, a round dance—applying, no doubt, to the rotation of the sun, which on this day begins afresh. Grimm, however, in his Mythology, makes out the name to be derived from the Latin Calendæ.

the Christian festival. The performers go about from house to house knocking at each door, with the usual formula, " Florile s'dalbe, buna sara lui Cracinim "—white is the flower, a happy Christmas night to you.

The *Turca*, or *Brezaia*, also belongs to the same category as the *Kolinda*, but is of a somewhat more boisterous character, and is performed by young men, who, all following a leader grotesquely attired in a long cloak and mask (oftenest representing the long beak of a stork, or a bull's head, hence the name), go about the villages night and day as long as the Christmas festivities last, pursuing the girls and terrifying the children. A certain amount of odium is attached to the personification of the Turca himself, and the man who has acted this part is regarded as unclean or bewitched by the devil during a period of six weeks, and may not enter a church nor approach a sacrament till this time has elapsed.

In the Bukovina the *Turca* or *Tur* goes by the name of the *Capra*, and is called *Cleampa* in the east of Transylvania.

4. The *Cantece de Irogi* is the name given to the text of many carnival games and dialogues in which *Rahula* (Rachel) and her child, a shepherd, a Jew, a Roumanian popa, and the devil, appear in somewhat unintelligible companionship.

5. The *Cantece de Stea*—songs of the star—are likewise sung at this period by children, who go about with a tinsel star at the end of a stick.

6. *The Plugul*—song of the plough—a set of verses sung on New Year's Day by young men fantastically dressed up, and with manifold little bells attached to feet and legs. They proceed noisily through the streets of towns and villages, cracking long whips as though urging on a team of oxen at the plough.

7. The *Cantece de Paparuga* are songs which are sung on the third Sunday after Easter, or in cases of prolonged drought.

8. The *Cantece de Nunta* are the wedding songs, of which there are a great number. These are, however, rarely sung, but oftener recited. They take various forms, such as that of invitation, health drinking, congratulations, &c. To these may be added the *Cantece de Cumetrie* and the *Cantecul ursitelor*, which express rejoicings over a new-born infant.

9. The *Descantece* or descantations are very numerous. They consist in secret charms or spells expressed in rhyme, which, in order to be efficacious, must be imparted to children or grandchildren only when the parent is lying on his deathbed. These oftenest relate to illnesses of man or beast, to love or to life; and each separate

contingency has its own set formula, which is thus transmitted from generation to generation.

10. The *Bocete* are songs of mourning, usually sung over the corpse by paid mourners.

On the principle that the character of a people is best demonstrated by its proverbs, a few specimens of those most current among Roumanians may be here quoted :—

" A man without enemies is of little value."

" It is easier to keep guard over a bush full of live hares than over one woman."

" A hen which cackles overnight lays no egg in the morning."

" A wise enemy is better than a foolish friend."

" In the daytime he runs away from the buffalo, but in the night he seizes the devil by the horn." [1]

" Carry your wife your whole life on your back, but, if once you set her down, she will say, ' I am tired.' "

" The just man always goes about with a bruised head."

" Sit crooked, but speak straight."

" Father and mother you will never find again, but wives as many as you list."

---

[1] The meaning of this I take to be, that the dangers we recognise and run away from are smaller than those we encounter without knowing it.

" The blessing of many children has broken no man's roof as yet."

" Better an egg to-day than an ox next year."

" No one throws a stone at a fruitless tree."

" Patience and silence give the grapes time to grow sweet."

" If you seek for a faultless friend you will be friendless all your life."

" There where you cannot catch anything, do not stretch out your hand."

" Who runs after two hares will not even catch one."

" The dog does not run away from a whole forest of trees, but a single stick will make him run."

" A real Jew will never pause to eat until he has cheated you."

" You cannot carry two melons in one hand."

" Who has been bitten by a snake is afraid of a lizard."

CHAPTER XXIII.

ROUMANIAN POETRY.

IT is hardly necessary to remark that the history of Roumanian literature must needs be a scanty one as yet. Considering the past history of these people on either side of the frontier, and the manner in which they have been oppressed and persecuted, the wonder is rather to find them to-day so far advanced on the road that leads to immortality.

The first Roumanian book (a collection of psalms, probably translated from the Greek) was printed at Kronstadt in 1577, and was succeeded by many other similar works, all printed in Cyrillian characters.

As historians and chroniclers, the names of Ureki, Miron Kostin, Dosithei, and of Prince Dimetrie Kantemir, all hold honourable positions between the end of the sixteenth and the beginning of the eighteenth century. Political events then stemmed

the current of progress for a time, and made of the
rest of the eighteenth century a period of intellec-
tual stagnation for all Roumanians, whether of
Wallachia, Moldavia, or Transylvania.   It was
from the latter country that about the year 1820
was given the first impulse towards resurrection,
connected with which we read the names of Lazar,
Majorescu, Assaki, Mikul, Petru Major, Cipariu,
Bolinteanu, Balcescu, Constantin Negruzzi, and
Cogalnitscheanu.

It was only after the middle of the present century that Latin characters began to be adopted in
place of Cyrillian ones, and indeed it is not easy to
understand why the Cyrillian alphabet ever came
to be used at all. On this subject Stanley, writing in 1856, speaks as follows :—

"The Latinity of Rouman is, however, sadly
disguised under the Cyrillic alphabet, in which it
has hitherto been habited.   This alphabet was
adopted about 1400 A.D., after an attempt by one
of the Popes to unite the Roumans to the Catholic
Church.   The priests then burned the books in the
Roman or European letters, and the Russians have
opposed all the attempts made latterly to cast off
the Sclavonic alphabet, by which the Rouman
language is enchained and bound to the Sclavonic
dialects. . . . The difficulty of coming to an

agreement among the men of letters as to the system to be adopted for rendering the Cyrillic letters by Roman type, has retarded this movement as much, perhaps, as political opposition."

The first Roumanian political newspaper was issued by Georg Baritin in 1838. At present several Roumanian newspapers appear in Transylvania, of which the ' Observatorul ' and the ' Telegraful Roman ' are the principal ones. There are in the country two Greek Catholic seminaries for priests, and one Greek Oriental one, a commercial school at Kronstadt, four upper gymnasiums, and numerous primary schools, all of which are self-supporting, and receive no assistance from the Hungarian Government.

Some portion of the rich store of folk songs which from time immemorial have been sung in the country by wandering minstrels, called *cantari*, has been rescued from oblivion by the efforts of Alexandri, and after him Torceanu, who, going about from village to village, have written down all they could learn from the lips of the peasants. One of the most beautiful and pathetic of the ballads thus collected by Alexandri is that of Curte d'Arghisch, an ancient and well-known Roumanian legend, the greater part of which I have here endeavoured to reproduce in an English version. These ballads are, however, exceedingly difficult to translate at all characteristically, our language neither possessing that abundant choice of rhyme, so apt to drive a translator to envious despair, nor yet the harmonious current of sound which lends a peculiar charm to the loose and rambling metre in which these songs are mostly written.

CLOISTER ARGHISCH.

I.

By the Arghisch river,
By the bonny brim,
Goes the Voyvod Negru,[1]
Other ten with him.
Nine of these his comrades,
Master masons be,
And the tenth is Manoll,
Masters' master he.
And the ten are questing,
Where along the tide
They shall build the minster,
And their fame beside.

---

[1] The Hospodar Negru, or Nyagon as he is sometimes called, reigned from 1513 to 1521. Long detained as hostage at the court of Sultan Selim I., he had the opportunity of studying oriental architecture, and himself directed the building of a celebrated mosque which had, we are told, no less than 999 windows and 366 minarets. This edifice so delighted the Sultan that he set Nyagon at liberty, presenting him with all the rich materials remaining over from the building of the mosque, in order to erect a church in his native country. Returning thither, he is said to have brought with him the celebrated architect Manoll, or Manolli, by birth a Phanariot, who, with his wife Annika, is immortalised in this ballad.

ROUMANIAN POETRY.   279

Then as on they stray,
Meets them on the way
A shepherd lad, that ditty sad
Upon his pipe doth play.

"Shepherd lad, dear shepherd lad,
Mournful ditty playing,
Up the river has thy flock
And hast thou been straying?
Down have strayed both thou and they,
Down along the river?
In thy wanderings where hast been,
Say, hast thou a building seen
Standing by the river,
Built of moss-grown ancient stone,
All unfinished and alone,
Where the hazels, green and lank,
Shoot amid the copsewood dank?"

"Ay, my master, that have I
Sighted as I wandered by;
Sooth, a wall doth on the strand
Lonely and unfinished stand,
At whose sight my hounds in haste
Howling fled across the waste!"

When this word the Prince had heard,
Joyful man was he:
"Haste away! come, no delay,
Haste thee instantly;
These, my master masons nine,
Lead unto yon wall,
And Manoll the tenth, that is
Master of them all."

"See ye yonder wall of mine?
Know that here the spot I name
For the sacred cloister's shrine,
For my everlasting fame.
Now, ye mighty masters all,
Fellows of the builder's craft,

Haste away ! night and day
Raise ye, build ye, roof and wall.
Build a cloister worthy me,
Such as never men did see:
Fail to build it as I say,
I will build you instantly,
Build you living, every one,
'Neath the pile's foundation-stone."

II.

Hastily with line and rule
Work they out the cloister's plan ;
Hastily with eager tool
Delve foundations in the sod,
Where shall stand the house of God.
Never resting night or day,
Building, ever building, they
Hurry on the work alway.
But what in the day has grown,
In the night is overthrown.
Next day, next, and next again,
What within the hours of light
They have reared with toil and pain,
Falls to ruin in the night,
And all labour is in vain ;
For the pile will not remain,
Falling nightly down again.

Wondering and wrathful then
Doth the Prince the builders call,
Raging, threatens once again
He will build them, build them all,
Build them in beneath the wall.
And the master builders nine,
Thus, their wretched lives at stake,
Quaking toil, and toiling quake,
All throughout the summer light,
Till the day gives way to night.

But Manoll upon a day
Puts the irksome task away,

Lays him down to sleep, and thus
Dream he dreameth marvellous,
Which, awak'ning from repose,
Straightway doth he then disclose :

" Hear my story, masters mine,
Ye my fellow craftsmen nine ;
Hearken to me while I tell
Dream in sleep that me befell :
From the height of heaven clear
Was it borne upon my ear.
Ever we shall build in vain,
Crumbling still our work again,
Till together swear we all
To immure within the wall
Her who at the peep of day
Chances first to come this way
Hither, who is sent by fate,
Bearing food for swain or mate,
Wife or sweetheart though it be,
Maid or matron equally.
Therefore listen, comrades mine :
Would you build this holy shrine,—
Would you to enduring fame
Evermore transmit your name,—
Vow we all a solemn vow,
As we stand together now,
Whosoever it shall be
That his lovèd one shall see,
Chancing here her way to take
When the morrow's light doth break,
Will as victim bid her fall,
Buried living in the wall ! "

III.

Smiling doth the morning break ;
With the dawn Manoll, awake,
Scaling the enclosure's bound,
Mounts the scaffold ; all around,
Hill and dale, with glance of fear,
Anxious searcheth far and near.

What is this that greets his eyes ?
Who is it that hither hies ?
'Tis his wife he doth behold,
Sweetest blossom of the wold ;
She it is that hasteth here,
Bringing for her husband dear
Meat and wine his heart to cheer.

Sure too awful is the sight !
Can his senses witness right ?
Leaps his heart and reels his brain
In an agony of pain.
Then on bended knees he falls,
Desperate on heaven calls—

      " O Lord my God,
         That rul'st on high,
      Ope Thou the flood-gates
         Of the sky ;
      Down upon earth
         Thy torrents pour,
      Till brook and river
         Rise and roar,
      Till raging floods
         My wife shall stay,
      Shall turn her back
         The homeward way ! "

Lo ! in pity God has hearkened—
That which he has asked is done :
Clouds the heaven's face have darkened,
They have blotted out the sun ;
Down the rains in torrents pour,
Brook and river rage and roar.
But nor storm nor flood can stay
Manoll's wife upon her way :
Pressing onwards, halting never,
Plunging through the foaming river,
Knowing nought of doubt or fear,
Near she hasteth, and more near.

The poem goes on to say how Manoll a second time implores the Creator to send a hurricane which shall ravage the face of nature and impede her progress. Once more his prayer is granted, and a mighty wind, which,—

> Sighing loud and moaning,
> Thundering and droning,
> Down the plane-trees bending,
> And the pines uprending,—

rages over the land.

> But no earthly force
> Checks her steady course,
> And all vainly passed
> By the furious blast,
> In the storm she quavers,
> But yet never wavers,
> And, oh hapless lot!
> Soon has reached the spot.

The fourth canto relates how the nine master masons are filled with joy at sight of this heaven-sent victim. Manoll alone is sad, as, kissing his wife, he takes her in his arms and carries her up the scaffolding. There he places her in a niche, explaining that they are going to pretend to build her in merely as a joke; while the poor young wife, scenting no danger, claps her hands in childish pleasure at the idea.

> But her spouse, with gloomy face,
> Speaks no word, and works apace:
> Of his dream he thinks alone,
> As they pile up stone on stone.

And the church walls upwards shoot,
Cover soon her dainty foot,
Reaching then above the knee;
Where is vanished all her glee?
As, becoming deadly pale,
Thus the wife begins to wail:

    "Manolli, dear Manolli!
    Master, master Manolli!
    Prithee, now this joking cease,
    And thy wife from here release;
    See, the wall is closing fast,
    In its grip am I compassed.
    Manolli, dear Manolli!
    Master, master Manolli·!"

But Manoll makes no reply,
Works with restless energy.
Higher and yet higher
Grows the wall entire,
Grows with lightning haste,
Reaches soon her waist,
Reaches soon her breast;
She no more can jest,
Hardly can she speak,
With voice faint and weak:

    "Manolli, dear Manolli!
    Master, master Manolli!
    Stop this joke and set me free,—
    Soon a mother shall I be;
    See, the wall is crushing me,
    These hard stones my babe will kill;
    With salt tears my bosom fill."

But Manoll makes no reply,
Works with restless energy.
Higher and yet higher
Grows the wall entire;
O'er her dainty foot
Fast the church walls shoot;

Fair Annika's knee
Soon no more they see,
Building on in haste
To her lithesome waist;
Hidden is her breast,
By the stones compressed;
Hidden now her eye,
As the wall grows high;
Building on apace,
Hidden soon her face!
And the hapless woman, she
Laughs no longer now in glee,
But from out the cruel wall
Still the feeble voice doth call:

" Manolli, dear Manolli!
Master, master Manolli!
See the wall is closing quite,
Vanished the last ray of light."

There is still a fifth canto to this ballad, but of such decidedly inferior merit as to suggest the idea that it is a piece of patchwork added on at a later period. The prince, delighted at the success of the building, asks the master masons whether they could undertake to raise a second church of yet nobler, loftier proportions than the first? This question being answered in the affirmative, the tyrannical Vayvod, probably afraid of their embellishing some other country with the work of their genius, orders the ladders and scaffolding to be removed from the building, so that the ten illustrious architects are left standing on the roof, there to perish of starvation. Hoping to escape this doom, each of the master masons constructs for himself a pair of artificial wings, or rather a sort of parachute, out of light wooden shingles, and by means of which he hopes safely to reach the ground. But the parachutes are a miserable failure, and crashing down with violence, the nine master masons are turned into as many stones. Manoll, the last to descend, and distracted at hearing the wailing voice of his dying wife calling upon him, falls likewise; but the tears welling up from his breast, cause him to be transformed into a spring of crystal water flowing near the church, and to this day known by the name of Manolli's well.

"Miora," or "The Lamb," is another popular ballad, which, sung and recited throughout Roumania and Transylvania, is gracefully illustrative of the idyllic bond by which shepherd and flock are united :—

MIORA.

Where the mountains open, there
Runs a pathway passing fair,
And along this flowery way
Shepherds came one summer day.
      Snowy flocks were three,
      Led by shepherds three.
One from Magyarland had come,
Wrantscha was another's home,
From Moldavia one had come;
But the one from Magyarland,
And from Wrantscha—hand in hand,

Council held they secretly,
And resolved deceitfully,
    When behind the hill
    Sank the sun, to kill
The Moldavian herd, for he
Was the richest of the three.
    Strongest were his rams,
    Fattest were his dams,
    Whitest were his lambs,
And his dogs the fiercest,
And his horse the fleetest.

But a lambkin white,
With eyes soft and bright,
Since the break of day
Bleats so piteously,
Does not cease to bleat,
No more grass will eat.

"Little lambkin white,
Thou my favourite,
Why since break of day
Bleat so piteously?
Never cease to bleat,
No more grass wiltst eat.
O my lambkin sweet,
Wherefore dost complain?
Say, dost suffer pain?"

"Gentle shepherd, master dear,
Prithee but my warning hear;
Lead away thy flock of sheep
Where the woodland shades are deep;
There in peace can we abide,—
Forests dense there are to hide.
Shepherd, shepherd! list to me;
Call thy dog to follow thee;
Choose the fiercest one of all,
Ear most watchful to thy call,
For the other herds have sworn
Thou shalt die before the morn!"

"Little lamb, if true dost say,
Hast the gift to prophesy,
And if it must come to pass
That I thus shall die, alas !
Is it written that my life
Thus shall end a cruel knife,
Tell the shepherds where to lay
My cold body in the clay.
　　Near unto my sheep
　　Would I wish to sleep,
　　From the grave to hark
　　When the sheep-dogs bark.
　　On the mound I pray
　　Three new flutes to lay :
One of beechwood fine be made,
Sings of love that cannot fade ;
One carved out of whitest bone,
For my broken heart makes moan ;.
One of elder wood let be,
For its tones are proud and free.
　　When at evenfall
　　'Gin the winds to call,
　　List'ning to the sound,
　　Gather then around
　　All my faithful sheep,
　　Bloody tears to weep.
　　But that I am dead
　　Let no word be said :
　　Tell them that a queen
　　Passing fair was seen,
　　Took me for her mate ;
　　That we sit in state
　　On a lofty throne ;
　　That the sun and moon
　　Held the golden crown,
　　And a star fell down
　　Straight above my head.
　　Say, when I was wed,
　　Oak-tree, beech, and pine,
　　All were guests of mine

At the wedding-feast;
And the holy priest
Was a mountain high.
Made sweet melody
Thousand birds from near and far,
Every torch a golden star.
But if thou shouldst meet,
Oh! if thou shouldst meet,
A poor haggard matron,
Torn her scarlet apron,
Wet with tears her eyes,
Hoarse with choking sighs,
'Tis my mother old,
Running o'er the wold,
Asking every one,
"Have you seen my son?
In the whole land none
Other was so fair,
With such raven hair,
Soft to feel as silk;
Like the purest milk,
None had skin so white;
None had eyes so bright,
As a pair of sloes.
And where'er he goes,
Shepherd none there be
Half so fair as he!"
Lamb, oh pity take,
Else her heart will break.
Tell her that a queen
Passing fair was seen,
Took me for her mate;
That we sit in state
On a lofty throne;
That the sun and moon
Held the golden crown,
And a star fell down
Straight above my head.
Say, when I was wed,
Oak-tree, beech, and pine,
All were guests of mine

> At the wedding feast;
> And the holy priest
> Was a mountain high.
> Made sweet melody
> Thousand birds from near and far,
> Every torch a golden star."[1]

The third and last of those folk songs which limited space permits me here to quote, is one I have selected as being peculiarly characteristic of the tender and clinging affection these people bear to their progeny.   Devoid of poetical merit it may perhaps be, but surely the unsatisfied yearnings of a childless woman have seldom been more pathetically rendered?

The Roumanian's Desire.

> Would it but th' Almighty please
> This my yearning heart to ease,
> But to send a little son,
> Little cherub for mine own.
>
> All the day and all the night
> Would I rock my angel bright;
> Gently shielded it should rest
> Ever on my happy breast.
>
> I would feed it, I would tend it,
> From each peril I'd defend it;
> Whisp'ring with the voice of love,
> Suck, my chick, my lamb, my dove.

---

[1] A prose translation of this poem appeared in Stanley's 'Rouman Anthology,' 1856.

Did but heaven hear my voice,
Evermore would I rejoice;
Golden gift so bright and rare,
Little baby soft and fair.

Love that on him I'd bestow,
Other child did never know;
Such his loveliness and worth,
Ne'er was like him child on earth.

Lips like coral, skin like snow,
Eyes like those of mountain roe;
And the roses on his cheek,
Elsewhere you in vain would seek.

Mouth so sweet, and eyes so bright,
Would I kiss from morn to night;
Kiss his cheek and kiss his hair,
Singing, "How my child is fair!"

Every holy prayer I know
Should secure my child from woe;
Every magic herb I'd pluck,
For to bring him endless luck.[1]

Surely then he'd grow apace,
Strong of limb and fair of face,
And a hero such as he
Earth before did never see!

It is not easy to classify the cultivated Roumanian writers of the present day, still less so is it to select appropriate specimens from their works. Roumanian literature is in a transition state at present, and, despite much talent and energy on the part of its representatives, has not as yet regained any fixed national character. Perhaps,

[1] This allusion to prayer and magic in the same breath is thoroughly characteristic of the Roumanian's religion.

indeed, it would be more correct to say that precisely the talent and energy of some of the most gifted writers have harmed Roumanian literature more than they have assisted it, by dragging into fashion a dozen different modes utterly incongruous with each other, and with the mainsprings of Roumanian thought and feeling. No doubt the custom of sending their children to be educated outside the country is much to blame for this; and naturally enough, French poets have been imported into the land along with Parisian fashions.

Béranger and Musset, along with Shakespeare, Goethe, Byron, and Heine, have all been abused in this manner, by men who should have understood that the strength of any literature does not lie in the successful imitation of foreign models, however excellent, but rather in the intelligent exploitation of its own historical and artistic treasures. Even Basil Alexandri, the first and most national of Roumanian poets, sometimes falls unconsciously into this error, still more perceptible in the works of Rosetti, Negruzzi, and Cornea.

Odobescu, Gane, Alexi, and Dunca have acquired some fame as writers of fiction; and Joan Slavici in particular may here be cited for his charming sketches of rural life, which have something of the force and delicacy of Turguenief's hand.

FET LOGOFET [1] (*literally*, YOUNG FOOLHARDY).

Thou radiant young knight,
With glance full of light,
  With golden-locked hair,
Oh, turn thy proud steed;
Of the forest take heed—
  The dragon lies there.

Thou fairest of maids,
With silken-like braids,
  So slender thy zone,
My good sword will pierce
The monster so fierce,
  And fear I have none.

Thou wrestler, thou ranger,
Thou seeker of danger,
  With eyes flashing fire;
Thy fate will be dolesome;
The dragon is loathsome,
  And fearful his ire.

Thou coaxer, thou pleader,
Thou sweet interceder,
  My star silver bright!
Both dragon and drake,
Before me they quake,
  And fly at my sight.

Thou stealer of hearts,
With golden-tipped darts,
  Yet list to my cry!
Thou canst not escape,
His open jaws gape,
  Turn water to sky!

Thou angel-like child,
With blue eyes so mild,

----

[1] By B. Alexandri.

Yet needst not to sigh;
For this my good steed
The wind can outspeed,
   And rear heaven-high!

Oh, radiant young knight,
With eyes full of light,
   That masterful shine,
Oh, hark to my prayer,
And do not go there;
   My heart it is thine!

Yet needs I must ride
To win as my bride
   Thou, maiden most sweet;
I must gain renown—
Either death or a crown—
   To lay at thy feet.

THE FAULT IS NOT THINE.[1]

Full oft hast thou sworn that on this side the grave
Thy love and thy heart should for ever be mine;
But thou hast forgotten, and I—I forgave,
For such is the world, and the fault is not thine.

And again was thy cry, " Thou belov'd of my heart,
In heaven itself, without thee I'd pine! "
On earth still we dwell—yet dwell we apart;
'Tis the fault of our age, and the fault is not thine.

My arms they embraced thee, I drank with delight
The dew from thy lips like a nectar divine;
But the dew turned to venom, its freshness to blight,
For such is thy sex, and the fault is not thine.

Thy love and thine honour, thy virtue and troth,
Given now to another, were yesterday mine;
Thou knowest not Love! then why should I be wroth?
'Tis the fault of thy race, and the fault is not thine.

---

[1] By K. A. Rosetti.

Far stronger than Love were both riches and pride,
And swiftly and surely thy faith did decline;
Thy wounds they are healed, thy tears they are dried,
Thou couldst not remember—the fault is not thine.

Yet though thou art faithless, and falsely hast left me,
My eyes can see nought but an angel divine;
My heart flutters wildly whenever I see thee—
'Tis the fault of my love, and the fault is not mine!

I do not suppose that any one with the slightest knowledge of Roumania and Roumanians can fail to detect an alien note in both these compositions, despite the grace of the originals; nor can one help feeling that these authors should have been capable of far better things.

And surely far better and grander things will come ere long from this nation, at once so old and so young! when, having regained its lost self-confidence, it comes to understand that more evil than good is engendered by a blind conformity to foreign fashions.

Already a step in the right direction has been taken in the matter of national dress, which, thanks to the praiseworthy example of the Roumanian queen, has lately received much attention. And as in dress, so in literature, does Carmen Sylva take the lead, and endeavour to teach her people to value national productions above foreign importations.

When, therefore, Roumanian writers begin to see

that their force lies not in the servile imitation of Western models, but in working out the rich vein of their own folk-lore, and in bridging over the space which takes them back to ancient pagan traditions, then, doubtless, a new era will set in for the literature of the country. Let Roumanian poets leave Béranger and Musset to moulder on their bookshelves, and consign to oblivion Heinrich Heine, whose exquisitely morbid sentimentality is far too fragile an article to bear importation; let them cease from wandering abroad, and assuredly they will discover in their own forests and mountains better and more vigorous material than Paris or Germany can offer: the old stones around them will begin to speak, and the old gods will let themselves be lured from out their hiding-places. Then will it be seen that Apollo's lyre has not ceased to vibrate, and the lays of ancient Rome will arise and develop to new life.

CHAPTER XXIV.

THE ROUMANIANS : NATIONALITY AND ATROCITIES.

THE Roumanians have often been called slavish and cringing, but, considering their past history, it is not possible that they should be otherwise, oppressed and trampled on, persecuted, and treated as vermin by the surrounding races; and it should rather be matter for surprise that they have been able to continue existing at all under such a combination of adverse circumstances, which would assuredly have worn out a less powerful nature.

Until little more than a century ago, it was illegal for any Wallachian child to frequent a German or Hungarian school; while at that same period the Wallachian clergy were compelled to carry the Calvinistic bishop on their shoulders to and from his church, whenever he thought fit to exact their services. Still more inhuman was a law which continued in force up to the end of the sixteenth century, ordaining that each Wallachian out of the district of Poplaka, in the neighbourhood of Hermanstadt, who injured a tree, if only by peeling off the bark, was to be forthwith hung up to the same tree. " Should, however, the culprit remain undiscovered," prescribes the law, " then shall the community of Poplaka be bound to deliver up for execution some other Wallachian in his place."

The faults of the Roumanians are the faults of all slaves. Like all serfs they are lazy, not being yet accustomed to work for themselves, nor caring to work for a master : they have acquired cunning and deceit as the only weapons wherewith to meet tyranny and oppression. Sometimes, when goaded to passion, the Roumanian forgets himself, and his eyes flash fiercely on his tormentor ; but the gaze is instantly corrected, and the eyes lowered again to their habitual expression of abject humility.

Occasionally they have cast off the yoke and taken cruel revenge on their real or imaginary oppressors, as in 1848, when, instigated and stirred up by Austrian agents, they rose against their masters the Hungarian noblemen, and perpetrated atrocities as numerous as disgusting. They pillaged the country - houses, setting everything on fire, and put the nobles to death with many torturing devices, crucifying some and burying others up to the neck, cutting off tongues and plucking out eyes, as a diabolical fancy suggested.

This was all the more surprising, as the bond between serfs and masters had always been of a most peaceful and patriarchal character, and it was to his Hungarian landlord that the Wallachian had been always accustomed to turn for counsel or assistance. True, the serf was forced to pay certain tithes to his master; but in return, when ever the crops failed, the master himself was obliged to sustain the serf, and provide him with corn out of his own garneries.

A Hungarian lady related to me a very horrible instance of cruelty which had happened on the property of a near relation of her own in the revolution of 1848. This gentleman, one of the most generous and humane landlords, did not usually reside at his country-place, but had spent much time in foreign travel, and was unknown to most of his people, which, however, did not prevent them from resolving on his death. Hearing of the riots which had broken out on his estate, the nobleman was hastening to the spot; and the excited peasantry, informed of his impending arrival, prepared to receive him with scythes and pickaxes.

The servants of the household had all fled the neighbourhood at the first alarm; but there remained behind at the chateau the foster-daughter

of the gentleman, a girl of sixteen, who, brought
up with the family, was warmly attached to her
benefactor, whom she called father. Shutting herself up in a turret-room, she tremblingly awaited the
dénouement of the fearful drama which was being
enacted around her. From her window she could
overlook the road by which her foster-father was
expected to arrive, and she stood thus all day at
her post, straining her eyes for what she feared to
see, and praying God to keep her benefactor away.

Twilight had set in, and the moon began to
rise, when a solitary rider was at last descried
coming down the neighbouring hill. The poor
girl's heart sank within her, for she knew that this
could be no other than her father; and even had
she doubted it, the wild-beast roar which broke
from the peasants at the sight of their long-expected
prey destroyed all remnant of hope. As in a
horrible nightmare, she saw them advance towards
the horseman in a black heaving mass, like a crawl-
ing thunder-cloud, broken here and there by the
sinister gleam of a sharpened scythe. Paralysed
with horror, she yet was unable to look away, and
no merciful fainting-fit came to spare her the sight
of any of the horrible details which followed : how
the hapless rider was surrounded and speedily over-
powered ; how a dreadful scuffle ensued ; and after
an interval which seemed like an eternity, how

something was hoisted up at the end of a long pole —something round in shape and ghastly in hue— the head of her beloved benefactor!

By-and-by she was roused from her grief by the loud voices of rioters approaching, and presently the front door being shaken and forced in with a resounding crash, the bloody wretches proceeded to overrun the house, and ransack the larders and cellar, laying hands on whatever viands they could discover. In the large vaulted hall they began the carouse, seated round the banqueting-table, and on a platter in the centre was placed the head of their victim.

Two of the peasants who had been searching the upper apartments now appeared on the scene, dragging between them a convulsively trembling girl, who looked ready to die with terror. "They had found her up-stairs in the turret," they explained, "sobbing like a fool, and calling out for her father, like a suckling whelp that has lost its dam."

"The old man's daughter!" shouted one of the revellers; "let us cut off her head as well,—they will look fine together on the platter!"

"No," said another; "she is not worth killing, she is half dead already. Let her look at her dear father, since it is for him she is crying;"—and raising the dish from the table, he held it in horrible proximity to her shrinking face.

The poor girl tightly closed her eyes in order to
escape the dreadful sight, but her persecutors were
not inclined to let her off so easily. Maddened
alike by blood and drink, they grasped her roughly,
and seizing her long black eyelashes on either side,
by main force they compelled her to raise her eye-
lids and fix her swimming eyes on the gory head.

At first she could distinguish nothing for the
blinding tears which obscured her vision, but suddenly the mist cleared away, and the cry she
then uttered was so sharp and piercing that it
re-echoed again from the vaulted roof, and caused
the drinkers to pause for a minute, glass in hand.
Lucky it was for her and hers that the dull ear of
the tipsy murderers had failed to distinguish the
meaning of that cry aright, for in moments of
intense emotion widely different feelings are apt to
resemble each other in expression, so that joy may
be mistaken for grief, and hope for despair—and it
was hope, not despair, which had given that piercing sharpness to her voice, for the ghastly grinning
head before her was the head of a stranger !

The joyful exclamation rising to her lips was
checked just in time, as her dazed brain began to
recognise the urgency of the situation. She must
not undeceive these men, who were exulting over
the death of their landlord. Her father was not
dead, it is true, but neither was the danger yet

past, and his safety might depend on keeping up the delusion a little longer. By good-luck her confusion passed unnoticed by the semi-tipsy revellers, who presently had no more thought but for their bumpers, so that the young girl, enabled to creep away unobserved, was ultimately the means of saving the nobleman's life by sending a messenger to warn him of his danger.

The man who had been executed in his place turned out to be a gentleman from some neighbouring district, who in the dusk had taken a wrong turn on the road, thus occasioning the mistake which cost him his life.

Many such instances of cruelty, of which the Roumanians made themselves guilty in the year '48, have deprived them of the sympathy to which they might have laid claim as a suffering and oppressed race; but people who have a thorough knowledge of the Roumanian character, and are able to estimate correctly all the influences brought to bear on them at that time, do not hesitate to affirm that these people were far more sinned against than sinning, and cannot be held responsible for the atrocities they perpetrated. Even Hungarian nobles, themselves the greatest sufferers by all that occurred during the revolution, are wont to speak of them with a sort of pitying commiseration, as of

poor misguided creatures led astray by unscrupu-
lous agents, and wholly incapable of comprehend-
ing the heinousness of their behaviour.

An amusing illustration has been given of the
ignorance of these revolutionary peasants in 1848.
Some of them, having broken into a nobleman's
mansion, discovered a packet of old letters in a
drawer, and believing these to be patents of nobility, they proceeded to burn them in front of the
portrait of one of the family ancestors, exclaiming
tauntingly, "See, proud lord, how thy family becomes once more as ignoble as we ourselves are"!

Few races possess in such a marked degree the
blind and immovable sense of nationality which
characterises the Roumanians : they hardly ever
mingle with the surrounding races, far less adopt
manners and customs foreign to their own ; and it
is a remarkable fact that the seemingly stronger-
minded and more manly Hungarians are absolutely
powerless to influence them even in cases of intermarriage.   Thus the Hungarian woman who weds
a Roumanian husband will necessarily adopt the
dress and manners of his people, and her children
will be as good Roumanians as though they had no
drop of Magyar blood in their veins ; while the
Magyar who takes a Roumanian girl for his wife
will not only fail to convert her to his ideas, but
himself, subdued by her influence, will impercept-

ibly begin to lose his nationality. This is a fact well known and much lamented by the Hungarians themselves, who live in anticipated apprehension of seeing their people ultimately dissolving into Roumanians. This singular tenacity of the Roumanians to their own manners and customs is doubtless due to the influence of their religion, which teaches them that any deviation from their own established rules is sinful—which, as I have said before, is the whole pivot of Roumanian thought and action.

In some districts where an attempt was made in the time of Maria Theresa to replace the Greek popas by other clergymen belonging to the united faith, the inhabitants simply absented themselves from all church attendance or reception of the sacraments ; and there are instances on record of villages whose churches remained closed for over thirty years, because the people could not be induced to accept the change.

As to that portion of the Transylvanian Roumanians which in 1698 consented to embrace the united faith, their separation from their schismatic brethren is but a skin-deep one after all, having no influence whatsoever on their customs and superstitions, or on the strong bond of nationality which holds them all together.

It is a notable fact that among all oriental races

the ideas of religion and nationality are inextricably
bound together. So with the Roumanians, whose
language has no other word wherewith to express
religion or confession but *lege*, law—obviously derived from the Latin *lex*.

The deeply inrooted sense of Roumanian nationality has, moreover, received fresh stimulus in the
comprehension which of late years has been slowly
but surely dawning on the minds of these people—
that they are a nation like other nations, with a
right to be governed by a monarch of their own
choice, instead of being bandied about, backwards
and forwards, changing masters at each European
treaty. There is no doubt that the bulk of Roumanians living to-day in Hungary and Transylvania consider themselves to be serving in bondage,
and covertly gaze over the frontier for their real
monarch; and who can blame them for so doing?
In the many Roumanian hovels I have visited in
Transylvania, I have frequently come across the
portrait of the King of Roumania hung up in the
place of honour, but never once that of his Austrian
Majesty. Old woodcuts representing Michel the
Brave, the great hero of the Roumanians, and of
the rebel Hora,[1] are also pretty sure to be found

---

[1] The real name of this celebrated Wallachian rebel, born in 1740,
was Nykulaj Urszu. Under the reign of the Emperor Joseph II. he
became the chief instigator of a revolution among the sorely oppressed
Transylvanian Wallachs, who, rising to the number of 30,000 men,

adorning the walls of many a hut. It is likewise by no means uncommon to see village taverns bearing such titles as, " To the King of Roumania," or " To the United Roumanian Kingdom," &c.

A little incident which, taking place under my eyes, impressed me very strongly at the time, helped me to understand this feeling more clearly than I had done before. Two Roumanian generals engaged in some business regarding the regulation of the frontier, being at Hermanstadt for a few days, paid visits to the principal Austrian military authorities, and were the object of much courteous attention. One evening the Austrian commanding general had ordered the military band to play in honour of his Roumanian *confrères*, and seated along with them on the promenade, we were listening to the music. Presently two or three private soldiers passing by, stopped in front of us to stare at the foreign uniforms. Apparently their curiosity was not easily satisfied, for after five minutes had elapsed they still remained standing, as though rooted to the spot, and other soldiers had joined them as well, till the group soon numbered above a dozen heads.

proceeded to murder the Hungarian nobles, and plunder, sack, and burn their possessions. Hora's project was to raise himself to the position of sovereign, and he had already adopted the title of King of Dacia when he was captured, and, together with his confederate Kloska, very cruelly put to death at Karlsburg in 1785.

Being engaged in conversation, I did not at the
moment pay much attention to this circumstance,
but happening to turn round again some minutes
later, I was surprised to see that the spectators had
become doubled and quadrupled in the meantime,
and were steadily increasing every minute. Little
short of a hundred soldiers were now standing in
front of us, all gazing intently. Why were they
staring thus strangely? what were they looking
at? I asked myself confusedly, but luckily checked
the question rising to my lips, when it suddenly
struck me that *all* these men had swarthy complexions, and *each* one of them a pair of dark eyes,
and simultaneously I remembered that the infantry
regiment whose uniform they wore was recruited
from Roumanian villages round Hermanstadt.

They were perfectly quiet and submissive-looking,
betraying no sign of outward excitement or insub-
ordination; but their expression was not to be mistaken, and no attentive observer could have failed
to read its meaning aright. It was at *their own
generals* they were gazing in that hungry, longing
manner, and deep down in every dusky eye, piercing through a thick layer of patience, stupidity,
apathy, and military discipline, there smouldered
a spark of something vague and intangible, the
germ of a sort, of fire which has often kindled
revolutions and sometimes overturned kingdoms.

Heaven alone knows what was passing in the clouded brain of these poor ignorant men as they stood thus gaping and staring, in the intensity of their rapt attention! Visions of glory and freedom perchance, dreams of peace and of prosperity; dim far-off pictures of unattainable happiness, of a golden age to come, and an Arcadian state of things no more to be found on the dull surface of this weary world!

The Austrian generals tried not to look annoyed, the Roumanian generals strove not to look elated, and the English looker-on endeavoured (I trust somewhat more successfully) to conceal her amusement at the serio-comicality of the situation, which one and all we tacitly ignored with that exquisite hypocrisy characterising well-bred persons of every nation.

CHAPTER XXV.

THE ROUMANIANS : DEATH AND BURIAL—VAMPIRES
AND WERE-WOLVES.

NOWHERE does the inherent superstition of the
Roumanian peasant find stronger expression than
in his mourning and funeral rites, which are based
upon a totally original conception of death.

Among the various omens of approaching death
are the groundless barking of a dog, the shriek
of an owl, the falling down of a picture from the
wall, and the crowing of a black hen. The influence of this latter may, however, be annulled, and
the catastrophe averted, if the bird be put in a
sack and carried sunwise thrice round the dwell-
ing-house.

It is likewise prognostic of death to break off the
smaller portion of a fowl's merry-thought, to dream
of troubled water or of teeth falling out,[1] or to be
merry without apparent reason.

[1] Both Greeks and Romans attached an ominous meaning to a
dream of falling-out teeth.

A falling star always denotes that a soul is leaving the earth—for, according to Lithuanian mythology, to each star is attached the thread of some man's life, which, breaking at his death, causes the star to fall. In some places it is considered unsafe to point at a falling star.

A dying man may be restored to life if he be laid on Holy Saturday outside the church door, where the priest passing with the procession may step over him ; or else let him eat of a root which has been dug up from the churchyard on Good Friday : but if these and other remedies prove inefficient, then must the doomed man be given a burning candle into his hand, for it is considered to be the greatest of all misfortunes if a man die without a light—a favour the Roumanian durst not refuse to his deadliest enemy.

The corpse must be washed immediately after death, and the dirt, if necessary, scraped off with knives, because the dead man will be more likely to find favour above if he appear in a clean state before the Creator. Then he is attired in his best clothes, in doing which great care must be taken not to tie anything in a knot, for that would disturb his rest by keeping him bound down to the earth. Nor must he be suffered to carry away any particle of iron about his person, such as buttons, boot-nails, &c., for that would assuredly prevent him from reaching Paradise, the road to which is long, and, moreover, divided off by several tolls or ferries. To enable the soul to pass through these, a piece of money must be laid in the hand, under the pillow, or beneath the tongue of the corpse. In the neighbourhood of Forgaras, where the ferries or toll-bars are supposed to amount to twenty-five, the hair of the defunct is divided into as many plaits, and a piece of money secured in each. Likewise a small provision of needles, thread, pins, &c., is put into the coffin, to enable the pilgrim to repair any damages his clothes may receive on the way.

The family must also be careful not to leave a knife lying with the sharpened edge uppermost as long as the corpse remains in the house, or else the soul will be forced to ride on the blade.

The mourning songs, called *Bocete*, usually performed by paid mourners, are directly addressed to the corpse, and sung into his ear on either side. This is the last attempt made by the survivors to wake the dead man to life by reminding him of all he is leaving, and urging him to make a final effort to arouse his dormant faculties,—the thought which underlies these proceedings being that the dead man hears and sees all that goes on around him, and that it only requires the determined effort of a strong will in order to restore elasticity

to the stiffened limbs, and cause the torpid blood
to flow anew in the veins.

Here is a fragment of one of these mourning
songs, which are often very pathetic and fanciful :—

> " Mother dear, arise, arise,
> Dry the tearful household's eyes !
> Waken, waken from thy trance,
> Speak a word or cast a glance !
> Pity thou thy children's lot !
> Rise, O mother leave us not !
> Death triumphant, woe is me,
> From thy children snatcheth thee !
> To the wall hast turned thee now,
> Son nor daughter heedest thou.
> Laid the churchyard sod beneath,
> Thou shalt feel no breeze's breath
> On the surface of thy grave ;
> From thy brow shall grasses wave,
> From those eyes so mild and true
> Nodding harebells take their blue."

Women alone are allowed to take part in these
lamentations, and all women related to the deceased
by ties of blood or friendship are bound to assist
as mourners ; likewise, those whose families have
been on unfriendly terms with the dead man, now
appear to ask his forgiveness.

The corpse must remain exposed a full day and
night in the chamber of death, and during that
time must never be left alone, nor should the
lamentations be suffered to cease for a single
moment. For this reason it is customary to have
hired women to act the part of mourners, by re-

lieving each other at intervals in singing the mourning songs. Often the deceased himself, in his last testamentary disposition, has ordered the details of his funeral, and fixed the payment—sometimes very considerable—which the mourning women are to receive.

The men related to the deceased are also bound to spend the night in the house, keeping watch over the corpse. This is called keeping the *privegghia*, which, however, has not necessarily a mournful character, as they mostly pass the time with various games, or else seated at table with food and wine.

Before the funeral the priest is called in, who, reciting the words of the 50th Psalm, pours wine over the corpse. After this the coffin is closed, and must not be reopened unless the deceased be suspected to have died of a violent death, in which case the man accused of the crime is confronted with the corpse of his supposed victim, whose wounds will, at his sight, begin to bleed afresh.

In many places two openings corresponding to the ears of the deceased are cut in the wood of the coffin, to enable him to hear the songs of mourning which are sung on either side of him as he is carried to the grave. This singing into the ears has passed into a proverb, and when the Roumanian says, " *I-a-cantat la urechia* " (they have sung into his ear), it is tantamount to saying that prayer, advice, and remonstrance have all been used in vain.

Whoever dies unmarried must not be carried by married bearers to the grave : a married man or woman is carried by married men, and a youth by other youths, while a maiden is carried by other maidens with hanging dishevelled hair. In every case the rank of the bearer should correspond to that of the deceased, and a *fruntas* can as little be carried by *mylocasi*, as the bearers of a *codas* may be higher than himself in rank.

In many villages no funeral takes place in the forenoon, as the people believe that the soul will reach its destination more easily by following the march of the sinking sun.

The mass for the departed soul should, if possible, be said in the open air ; and when the coffin is lowered into the grave, the earthen jar containing the water in which the corpse has been washed must be shattered to atoms on the spot.

A thunderstorm during the funeral denotes that another death will shortly follow.

It is often customary to place bread and wine on the fresh grave - mound ; and in the case of young people, small fir-trees or gay-coloured flags are placed beside the cross, to which in the case of a shepherd a tuft of wool is always attached.

Seven copper coins, and seven loaves of bread

with each a lighted candle sticking in it, are often distributed to seven poor people at the grave. This also is intended to signify the tolls to be cleared on the way to heaven.

In some places it is usual for the procession returning from a funeral to take its way through a river or stream of running water, sometimes going a mile or two out of their way to avoid all bridges, thus making sure that the vagrant soul of the beloved deceased will not follow them back to the house.

Earth taken from a fresh grave-mound and laid behind the neck at night, will bring pleasant dreams; it may also serve as a cure against fever if made use of in the following manner: The person afflicted with fever repairs to the grave of some beloved relative, where, calling upon the defunct in the most tender terms, he begs of him or her the loan of a winding-sheet for a strange and unwelcome guest. Taking, then, from the grave a handful of earth, which he is careful to tie up tightly and place inside his shirt, the sick man goes away, and for three days and nights he carries this talisman about with him wherever he goes. On the fourth day he returns to the grave by a different route, and replacing the earth on the mound, thanks the dead man for the service rendered.

A still more efficacious remedy against fever is

to lay a string or thread the exact length of your own body into the coffin of some one newly deceased, saying these words, " May I shiver only when this dead man shivers." Sore eyes may be cured by anointing them with the dew gathered off the grass of the grave of a just man, on a fine evening in early spring ; and a bone taken from the deceased's right arm will cure boils and sores by its touch. Whoever would keep sparrows off his field, must between eleven o'clock and midnight collect earth from off seven different graves and scatter it over his field; while the same earth, if thrown over a dog addicted to hunting, will cure him of this defect.

The *pomeana* or funeral feast is invariably held after the funeral, for much of the peace of the defunct depends upon the strict observance of this ancient custom. All the favourite dishes of the dead man are served at this banquet, and each guest receives a cake, a jug of wine, and a wax candle in his memory. Similar *pomeanas* are repeated after a fortnight, six weeks, and on each anniversary of the death for the next seven years. On the first anniversary it is usual to bring bread and wine to the churchyard. The bread is distributed to the poor, and the wine poured down through the earth into the grave.

During six weeks after the funeral, the women of

318 THE LAND BEYOND THE FOREST.

the family let their hair hang uncombed and unplaited in sign of mourning. It is, moreover, no
uncommon thing for Roumanians to bind themselves down to a mourning of ten or twenty years,
or even for life, in memory of some beloved deceased
one. Thus in one of the villages there still lived,
two years ago, an old man who for the last forty
years had worn no head-covering, summer and
winter, in memory of his only son, who had died
in early youth.

In the case of a man who has died a violent
death, or in general of all such as have expired
without a light, none of these ceremonies take
place. Such a man has neither right to *bocete*,
privegghia, mass, or *pomeana*, nor is his body laid
in consecrated ground. He is buried wherever the
body may be found, on the bleak hillside or in the
heart of the forest where he met his death, his
last resting-place only marked by a heap of dry
branches, to which each passer-by is expected to
add by throwing a handful of twigs—usually a
thorny branch—on the spot. This handful of
thorns—*o mână de spini*, as the Roumanian calls
it—being the only mark of attention to which the
deceased can lay claim, therefore to the mind of
this people no thought is so dreadful as that of
dying deprived of light.

The attentions due to such as have received

orthodox burial often extend even beyond the seven first years after death ; for whenever the defunct appears in dream to any of the family, this likewise calls for another *pomeana,* and when this condition is not complied with, the soul thus neglected is apt to wander complaining about the earth, unable to find rest.

This restlessness on the part of the defunct may either be caused by his having concealed treasures during his lifetime, in which case he is doomed to haunt the place where he has hidden his riches until they are discovered ; or else he may have died with some secret sin on his conscience—such, for instance, as having removed the boundary stone from a neighbour's field in order to enlarge his own. He will then probably be compelled to pilger about with a sack of the stolen earth on his back. until he has succeeded in selling the whole of it to the people he meets in his nightly wanderings.

These restless spirits, called *strigoi,* are not malicious, but their appearance bodes no good, and may be regarded as omens of sickness or misfortune.

More decidedly evil is the *nosferatu* or vampire, in which every Roumanian peasant believes as firmly as he does in heaven or hell. There are two sorts of vampires, living and dead. The living vampire is generally the illegitimate offspring of two illegitimate persons ; but even a flawless pedigree will not ensure any one against the intrusion of a vampire into their family vault, since every person killed by a *nosferatu* becomes likewise a vampire after death, and will continue to suck the blood of other innocent persons till the spirit has been exorcised by opening the grave of the suspected person, and either driving a stake through the corpse, or else firing a pistol-shot into the coffin. To walk smoking round the grave on each anniversary of the death, is also supposed to be effective in confining the vampire. In very obstinate cases of *vampirism* it is recommended to cut off the head, and replace it in the coffin with the mouth filled with garlic; or to extract the heart and burn it, strewing its ashes over the grave.

That such remedies are often resorted to even now, is a well-attested fact, and there are probably few Roumanian villages where such have not taken place within memory of the inhabitants. There is likewise no Roumanian village which does not count among its inhabitants some old woman (usually a midwife) versed in the precautions to be taken in order to counteract vampires, and who makes of this science a flourishing trade. She is frequently called in by the family who has lost a member, and requested to "settle" the corpse securely in its coffin, so as to ensure it against wandering. The means by which she endeavours to counteract any vampire-like instincts which may be lurking are various. Sometimes she drives a nail through the forehead of the deceased, or else rubs the body with the fat of a pig which has been killed on the Feast of St Ignatius, five days before Christmas. It is also very usual to lay the thorny branch of a wild-rose bush across the body to prevent it leaving the coffin.

First cousin to the vampire, the long-exploded were - wolf of the Germans is here to be found lingering under the name of *prikolitsch*. Sometimes it is a dog instead of a wolf whose form a man has taken, or been compelled to take, as penance for his sins. In one village a story is still told—and believed—of such a man, who, driving home one Sunday with his wife, suddenly felt that the time for his transformation had come. He therefore gave over the reins to her, and stepped aside into the bushes, where, murmuring the mystic formula, he turned three somersaults over a ditch. Soon after the woman, waiting vainly for her husband, was attacked by a furious dog, which rushed barking out of the bushes and succeeded in biting her severely as well as tearing her dress. When, an hour or two later, the woman reached home after giving up her husband as lost, she was surprised to see him come smiling to meet her; but when between his teeth she caught sight of the shreds of her dress bitten out by the dog, the horror of this discovery caused her to faint away.

Another man used gravely to assert that for several years he had gone about in the form of a wolf, leading on a troop of these animals, till a hunter, in striking off his head, restored him to his natural shape.

This superstition once proved nearly fatal to a harmless botanist, who, while collecting plants on a hillside many years ago, was observed by some peasants, and, in consequence of his crouching attitude, mistaken for a wolf. Before they had time to reach him, however, he had risen to his feet and disclosed himself in the form of a man; but this in the mind of the Roumanians, who now regarded him as an aggravated case of wolf, was but additional motive for attacking him. They were quite sure that he must be a *prikolitsch*, for only such could change his shape in this unaccountable manner, and in another minute they were all in full cry after the wretched victim of science, who might have fared badly indeed had he not succeeded in gaining a carriage on the highroad before his pursuers came up.

I once inquired of an old Saxon woman whom I had visited with a view to extracting various pieces of superstitious information, whether she had ever come across a *prikolitsch* herself.

"Bless you!" she said, "when I was young there was no village without two or three of them at least, but now there seem to be fewer."

"So there is no *prikolitsch* in this village?" I asked, feeling particularly anxious to make the acquaintance of a real live were-wolf.

"No," she answered doubtfully—"not that I know of for certain, though of course there is no saying with those Roumanians. But close by here in the next street, round the corner, there lives the widow of a *prikolitsch* whom I knew. She is still a young woman, and lost her husband five or six years ago. In ordinary life he was a quiet enough fellow, rather weak and sickly-looking; but sometimes he used to disappear for a week or ten days at a time, and though his wife tried to deceive people by telling them that her husband was lying drunk in the loft, of course we knew better, for those were the times when he used to be away *wolving* in the mountains."

Thinking that the relict of a were-wolf was the next best thing to the were-wolf himself, I determined on paying my respects to the interesting widow; but on reaching her house the door was closed, and I had the cruel disappointment of learning that Madame Prikolitsch was not at home.

We do not require to go far for the explanation of the extraordinary tenacity of the were-wolf legend in a country like Transylvania, where real wolves still abound.   Every winter here brings fresh proof of the boldness and cunning of these terrible animals, whose attacks on flocks and farms are often conducted with a skill which would do honour to a human intellect.   Sometimes a whole village is kept in trepidation for weeks together by some particularly audacious leader of a flock of wolves, to whom the peasants not unnaturally attribute a more than animal nature ; and it is safe to prophesy that as long as the flesh-and-blood wolf continues to haunt the Transylvanian forests, so long will his spectre brother survive in the minds of the people.

CHAPTER XXVI.

ROUMANIAN SUPERSTITION : DAYS AND HOURS.

GRIMM has said that "superstition in all its multi-
fariousness constitutes a species of religion appli-
cable to all the common household necessities of
daily life;"[1] and if we view it as such, particular
forms of superstition may very well serve as guide
to the character and habits of the particular nation
in which they are prevalent. In Transylvania,
however, the task of classifying all the superstitions that come under our notice is a peculiarly
hard one, for perhaps nowhere else does this
curious crooked plant of delusion flourish so per-
sistently and in such bewildering variety as in
the land beyond the forest; and it would almost
seem as though the whole species of demons, pixies,
witches, and hobgoblins, driven from the rest of
Europe by the wand of science, had taken refuge

[1] "Der Aberglaube in seiner bunten Mannigfaltigkeit bildet ge-
wissermassen eine Religion für den ganzen neideren Hausbedärf."

within this mountain rampart, aware that here
they would find secure lurking-places whence to
defy their persecutors yet a while.

There are many reasons why such fabulous beings should retain an abnormally firm hold on
the soil of these parts, and looking at the matter
closely, we find no less than three distinct sources
of superstition :—

First, there is what may be called the indigenous
superstition of the country, the scenery of which
is particularly adapted to serve as background to
all sorts of supernatural beings. There are innumer-
able caverns whose depths seem made to harbour
whole legions of evil spirits ; forest glades, fit only
for fairy folk on moonlight nights ; solitary lakes,
which instinctively call up visions of water-sprites ;
golden treasures lying hidden in mountain chasms,
—all of which things have gradually insinuated themselves into the minds of the oldest inhabitants, the
Roumanians, so that these people, by nature imagin-
ative and poetically inclined, have built up for
themselves, out of the surrounding materials, a
whole code of fanciful superstition, to which they
adhere as closely as to their religion itself.

Secondly, there is here the imported superstition
—that is to say, the old German customs and beliefs
brought hither by the Saxon colonists from their
native land, and, like many other things, preserved

here in greater perfection than in the original country.

Thirdly, there is the influence of the wandering superstition of the gipsy tribes, themselves a race of fortune-tellers and witches, whose ambulatory caravans cover the country as with a network, and whose less vagrant members fill up the suburbs of towns and villages.

All these kinds of superstition have twined and intermingled, acted and reacted upon each other, so that in many cases it becomes a difficult matter to determine the exact parentage of some particular belief or custom ; but in a general way the three sources I have named may be admitted as a rough sort of classification in dealing with the principal superstitions here afloat.

Few races offer such an interesting field for research in their folk-lore as the Roumanians, in whose traditions we find side by side elements of Celtic, Slav, and Roman mythology,—a subject well worth a closer attention than it has hitherto received. The existence of the Celtic element has been explained by the assumption (believed by many historians to be well-founded), that as the present Roumanians are a mixed race originating in the fusion of Romans with Daciens, so were these latter themselves a complex nationality composed of Slav and Celtic ingredients.

The spirit of evil—or, not to put too fine a point on it, the devil—plays a conspicuous part in the Roumanian code of superstition, and such designations as *Gaura Draculuj*[1] (devil's hole), *Gregyna Draculuj* (devil's garden), *Jadu Draculuj* (devil's abyss), frequently found attached to rocks, caverns, and heights, attest that these people believe themselves to be surrounded on all sides by whole legions of evil spirits. These devils are furthermore assisted by *ismejus* (another sort of dragon), witches, and goblins, and to each of these dangerous beings are ascribed particular powers on particular days and at certain places. Many and curious are therefore the means by which the Roumanians endeavour to counteract these baleful influences ; and a whole complicated study, about as laborious as the mastering of an unknown language, is required in order to teach an unfortunate peasant to steer clear of the dangers by which he supposes himself to be beset on all sides. The bringing up of a common domestic cow is apparently as difficult a task as the rearing of any " dear gazelle," and even the well-doing of a

[1] *Dracu*, which in Roumanian does duty for the word devil, really means dragon ; as for devil proper, the word is wanting.

One writer, speaking of the Roumanians, observes that they swear by the dragon, which gives their oaths a painful sense of unreality.

simple turnip or potato about as precarious as that of the most tender exotic plant.

Of the seven days of the week, Wednesday (Miercuri) and Friday (Vinere) are considered suspicious days, on which it is not allowed to use needle or scissors, or to bake bread ; neither is it wise to sow flax on these days. No bargain should ever be concluded on a Friday; and Venus (here called Paraschiva), to whom the Friday is sacred, punishes all infractions of this rule by causing conflagrations.

Tuesday, however—or Marti, named from Mars, the bloody god of war—is a decidedly unlucky day, on which spinning is utterly prohibited ; and even such seemingly harmless actions as washing the hands and combing the hair are not unattended by danger. About sunset on Tuesday the evil spirit of that day is at its fullest force, and many people refrain from leaving their huts between sunset and midnight. " May the *mar sara* (spirit of Tuesday evening) carry you off ! " is here equivalent to saying, " May the devil take you ! "

It must not, however, be supposed that Monday, Thursday, and Saturday are unconditionally lucky days, on which the Roumanian is at liberty to do as he pleases. Thus every well-informed Roumanian matron knows that she may wash on Thursday and spin on Saturday, but that it would be a

fatal mistake to reverse the order of these proceedings; and though Thursday is a lucky day for
marriage, and is on that account mostly chosen for
weddings, it is proportionately unfavourable to
agriculture. In many places it is considered unsafe
to work in the fields on all Thursdays between
Easter and Pentecost, for it is believed that if these
days be not kept as days of rest, ravaging hailstorms will be the inevitable consequence. Many
of the more enlightened Roumanian popas have
preached in vain against this belief; and some
years ago the inhabitants of a village presented an
official complaint to the bishop, requesting the re-
moval of their popa, on the ground that he not
only gave scandal by working on the prohibited
days, but had actually caused them serious material
damage by the hailstorms his sinful behaviour had
provoked. This respect of the Thursday would
seem to be the result of a deeply rooted, though
now unconscious, worship of Jupiter (Joi), who
gives his name to the day.

To different hours of the day are likewise ascribed
different influences, favourable or the reverse.
Thus it is always considered unlucky to look at
one's self in the mirror after sunset; neither is it

<hr>

[1] This would seem to suggest a German or Scandinavian element
—the thunder-god Donar or Thor, who with his hammer confirms
unions.

wise to sweep dust over the threshold in the evening, or to restore a whip borrowed of a neighbour. The exact hour of noon is precarious because of the evil spirit *Pripolniza*, and so is midnight because of the *miase nopte* (night spirit), and it is safer to remain indoors at these hours. If, however, some misguided peasant does happen to leave his home at midnight, and espies (as very likely he may) a flaming dragon in the sky, he need not necessarily give himself up as lost, for if he have the presence of mind to stick a fork into the ground alongside of him, the fiery monster will thereby be prevented from carrying him off.

The advent of the new moon is always more or less fraught with danger, and nothing may be sown or planted at that time.

The Oriental Church has an abnormal number of feast-days, to each of which peculiar customs and superstitions are attached, a few of which may here find place.

On New Year's day it is customary for the Roumanian to interrogate his fate by placing a leaf of evergreen on the freshly swept and heated hearth-stone. If the leaf takes a gyratory movement, he will be lucky; but if it shrivels up where it lies,

¹ This spirit corresponds to the Polednice of the Bohemians and the Poludnica of Poles and Russians. Grimm, in speaking of the Russians in his 'German Mythology,' quotes from Boschorn's 'Resp. Moscov.': " Dæmonem quoque meridianum Moscovitæ et colunt."

then he may expect misfortune during the coming
year.[1] To ensure the welfare of the cattle, it is ad-
visable to place a gold or silver piece in the water-
trough out of which they drink for the first time
on New Year's morning.

The Feast of the Epiphany or Three Kings (*tre
crai*) is one of the oldest festivals, and was solem-
nised by the Oriental Church as early as the second
century. On this day, which popular belief regards
as the coldest in the winter, the blessing of the
waters, known as the Feast of the *Jordan* or *Bobe-
tasu* (baptism), takes place. The priests, attired in
full vestments, proceed to the shore of the nearest
river or lake, and there bless the waters, which have
been unclosed by cutting a Greek cross, some six
to eight feet long, in the ice. Every pious Roumanian is careful to fill a bottle with this consecrated water before the surface freezes over again,
and keeps it tightly corked and sealed up, as a
remedy in case of illness. On this day the principal food in most Roumanian houses consists of a
sort of jelly ; and in the evening the popa, coming
to each house in order to bless the cattle, which he
does by sprinkling holy water with a bunch of
wild basil-weed,[2] finds a table with food and drink

---

[1] Also practised by the Saxons.

[2] This plant, *Ocimum basilicum*, is much used by the Roumanians,
who ascribe to it both medicinal and magic properties.

awaiting him, from which a dish of boiled plums must never be wanting.

He who dies on that day is considered particularly lucky, for he will be sure to go straight to heaven, the gate of which is believed to stand open all day, in memory of the descent of the Holy Ghost at the baptism of Christ.

The Feast of St Theodore, 11th January (corresponding to our 23d January), is a day of rest for the girls, those transgressing this rule being liable to be carried off by the saint, who sometimes appears in the shape of a beautiful youth, sometimes in that of a terrible monster. No decent girl should leave her house unescorted on this day, for fear of the terrible Theodore. In some districts youths and maidens choose this day for swearing friendship, which bonds are inaugurated by a tree being hung over with little circular cakes, and danced round with songs and music, after which each cake is broken in two and divided between a youth and a maiden.

On the Wednesday in Holy Week the Easter loaves and cakes are baked, which next day are blessed, and some of the hallowed crumbs mixed

---

[1] The Serbs have also a corresponding day, called the Theodor Saturday, *Todoroma sumbota*, on which no work is done, on account of the Sintotere, a monster, half man half horse, who rides upon whoever falls in his power.

[2] Similar customs exist among the Hindoos, Slavs, and Serbs.

up with the cows' fodder. Woe to the woman who indulges in a nap to-day : for the whole year she will not be able to shake off her drowsiness. In the evening the young men bind as many wreaths as there are persons in their family, and each of these, marked with the name of an individual, is thrown up on the roof, the wreaths which fall to the ground indicating those who will die that year.

Skin diseases are cured by taking a bath on Good Friday in a stream or river which flows towards the east. This will not only cure the patient, but prevent the disease recurring within the year.[1]

In the night preceding Easter Sunday witches and demons are abroad, and hidden treasures are said to betray their site by a glowing flame. No God-fearing peasant will, however, allow himself to be tempted by the hope of such riches, which he cannot on that day appropriate without sin. He must not omit to attend the midnight church-service, and his devotion will be rewarded by the mystic qualities attached to the wax candle he has carried in his hand, and which, when lighted hereafter during a thunderstorm, will keep the lightning from striking his house.

The greatest luck which can befall a mortal is to be born on Easter Sunday, and this luck is increased if the birth take place at mid-day when

---

[1] Also believed by most Slav races.

the bells are ringing; but it is not lucky to die on that day.

Egg-shells are glued up against the doors, in memory of the Israelites, who anointed the doorposts with the lambs' blood at their flight from Egypt; and the wooden spoon with which the Easter eggs have been removed from the boiling-pot is carefully treasured up by each shepherd, for, worn in his belt, it gives him the power to distinguish the witches who seek to molest his flocks. Witches may also be descried by the man who on Easter Monday takes up his stand on a bridge above running water, remaining there from sunrise to sunset.

Perhaps the most important day in the Roumanian's year is St George, 24th April (6th May), the eve of which is said to be still frequently kept up by occult meetings taking place at night in lonely caverns or within ruined walls, and where all the ceremonies usual to the celebration of a witches' Sabbath are put into practice. This night is the great one to beware of witches, to counteract whose influence square - cut blocks of turf (to which are sometimes added thorny branches) are placed in front of each door and window.[1] This is supposed effectually to bar their entrance to house or stables, but for still greater

---

[1] Also usual in Moldavia.

precaution it is usual for the peasants to keep watch all night near the sleeping cattle. This same night is likewise the best one for seeking treasures.

The Feast of St George, being the day when most flocks are first driven out to pasture, is in a special manner the feast of all shepherds and cow-herds, and on this day only is it allowed for the Roumanian shepherd to count his flocks and assure himself of the exact number of sheep—these num-bers being, in general, but approximately guessed at and vaguely described. Thus, when interro-gated as to the number of his master's sheep, the Roumanian shepherd will probably inform you that they are as numerous as the stars of heaven, or as the daisies which dot the meadows.

The custom of throwing up wreaths on to the roof, as described above, is in some districts prac-tised on the Feast of St John the Baptist, 24th June (July 6th), instead of on the Wednesday in Holy Week. This is the day when the sun, having reached its zenith, begins its backward course (ac-cording to the people) with a trembling, dancing movement, in the same way as the sun is said to dance on Easter Sunday. The gateway of each house is decorated with a wreath of field-flowers; and at night fires lighted on the mountain-heights are supposed to keep away evil spirits from the

flocks. This custom of the St John fires is, however, to be found in many other countries, and is
undoubtedly a remnant of the old sun-worship
practised by Greeks, Romans, Scandinavians, Celts,
Slavs, Indians, Parsees, &c.

The Feast of St Elias, 20th July (August 1st), is
a very unlucky day, on which the lightning may be
expected to strike.[1] Every year—so we are told
in an ancient legend—St Elias appears in heaven
before the throne of the Almighty, and humbly
inquires when his feast-day is to be. He is invariably put off with divers excuses, being sometimes told that his feast-day has not yet come,
sometimes that the date for it is already past. At
this the saint grows angry, and wishing to punish
the human race for thus forgetting him, he hurls
down his thunderbolts upon the earth.

The Feast of St Spiridion, 13th December (January 24th), is an ominous day, especially for housewives, and this saint often destroys those who
desecrate his feast by manual labour.

That the cattle are endowed with speech during
the Christmas night is a general belief, but it is
not considered wise to pry upon them, or try to

[1] St Elias is also known in Servia as "Thunderer"; Bohemians and
Russians have a thunder-god named Perum; the Poles, Piorun; the
old Russians had Perkun, and the Lithuanians Perkunos,—all of
which may be assumed to be derived from the Indian sun-god, Sur-
jar or Mihirar, who, as personification of fire, is also named Perus.

overhear what they say, as the listener will rarely overhear any good. This night is likewise favourable to the discovery of hidden treasures, and the man who has courage to conjure up the Evil One will be sure to see him if he call upon him at midnight. Three burning coals placed on the threshold will prevent the devil from carrying him off.

A round cake baked at Christmas goes by the name of the *rota* (wheel), and is probably symbolic of the sun's rotation.

The girl whose thoughts are turned towards love and matrimony, has many approved methods of testing her fate on the New Year's night. First of all, she may, by cracking her finger-joints, accurately ascertain the number of her admirers; also a fresh-laid egg broken into a glass of water will give much clue to the events in store for her by the shape it assumes; and a swine's bristle stuck in a straw and thrown on the heated hearthstone, is reliable as a talisman which disperses love or jealousy.[1] To form a conjecture as to the figure and build of her future husband, she is recommended to throw an armful of firewood as far as

---

[1] Swine have been regarded as sacred animals by various people, which is probably the explanation of the German expression of *Sauglück* (sow's-luck), and of the *Glückschweinchen* (little luck-pigs) which have lately become fashionable as charms to hang to the watch-chain.

she can backwards over her shoulder : the piece which has gone farthest will be the image of her intended, according as the stick happens to be long or short, broad or slender, straight or crooked.

Another such game is to place on the table a row of earthen pots upside down. Under each of these is concealed something different—as corn, salt, wool, coals, or money—and the girl is desired to make her choice : thus money stands for a rich husband, and wool for an old one; corn signifies an agriculturist, and salt connubial happiness, but coals are prophetic of misfortune.

If these general indications do not suffice, and the maiden desire to see the reflection of her bridegroom's face in the water, she has only to step naked at midnight into the nearest lake or river; or if she not unnaturally shrink from this chilly oracle, let her take her stand on the more congenial dunghill, with a piece of Christmas cake in her mouth, and, as the clock strikes twelve, listen attentively for the first sound of a dog's bark which reaches her ear. From whichever side it proceeds will also come the expected suitor.

It is likewise on the last day of the year that the agriculturist seeks a prognostic of the weather for the coming year, by making what is called the onion calendar, which consists in putting salt into twelve hollowed-out onions and giving to each the name of a month. Those onions in which the salt has melted by the following morning will be rainy months.[1]

[1] Also practised by the Saxons.

END OF THE FIRST VOLUME.

PRINTED BY WILLIAM BLACKWOOD AND SONS.

Made in the USA
Monee, IL
10 December 2021

84740798R00215